HOW TO LICENSE YOUR MILLION DOLLAR IDEA

HOW TO LICENSE YOUR MILLION DOLLAR IDEA

CASH IN ON YOUR INVENTIONS, NEW PRODUCT IDEAS, SOFTWARE, WEB BUSINESS IDEAS, **AND MORE**

THIRD EDITION

HARVEY REESE

WILEY

John Wiley & Sons, Inc.

Published by John Wiley & Sons, Inc., Hoboken, New Jersey.

Published simultaneously in Canada.

For general information on our other products and services or for technical support, please contact our Customer Care Department within the United States at (800) 762-2974, outside the United States at (317) 572-3993 or fax (317) 572-4002.

Wiley also publishes its books in a variety of electronic formats. Some content that appears in print may not be available in electronic books. For more information about Wiley products, visit our website at www.wiley.com.

Library of Congress Cataloging-in-Publication Data:

Reese, Harvey.
    How to license your million dollar idea: cash in on your inventions, new product ideas, software, web business ideas, and more/Harvey Reese.—3rd ed.
        p. cm.
    Includes index.
    ISBN 978-1-118-02242-9 (pbk); ISBN 978-1-118-08784-8 (ebk);
    ISBN 978-1-118-08785-5 (ebk); ISBN 978-1-118-08786-2 (ebk)
        1. Patent laws and legislation—United States—Popular works.   2. Inventions—United States.   I. Title.
    KF3114.85.R44 2011
    346.7304'86—dc22

                                                                                2011005892

Printed in the United States of America
10 9 8 7 6 5 4 3 2 1

CONTENTS

Success is just a matter of luck.
Ask any failure.
—Earl Wilson

PREFACE

If you are a reader of one of the previous editions of this book, I welcome you back. You'll find a great deal of fresh, helpful new material has been added to justify your revisit. All of the information, facts, and resources have been brought up to date, as have the contracts and forms in the Appendix. However, the real difference is this new edition's expanded view of what constitutes a "million dollar idea." Now that the electronics revolution is so well established as part of our everyday lives, it has opened up all sorts of wonderful new licensing opportunities for creative minds like yours that didn't widely exist when the former edition was published. But wow! They sure do now!

It's great if you have an idea for a new cookie cutter or a garden tool invention—but you might just as easily have an idea for a new software application, or a new TV game show, or a new reality TV show, or even an idea for a new website business. Fresh and original ideas like these are no less valuable if properly prepared and placed in the right hands. A royalty check is still a royalty check, no matter what category of brilliant idea earned it.

However, if you want to run with the big dogs, you have to know what to do and how to do it—and that's what this edition will show you. In addition to new instructional information for the more familiar kinds of product inventions, this new edition addresses these other types of intellectual property ideas as well, step by step, page by page, chapter by chapter. In most instances the essential process is almost identical. Whatever the idea, and allowing for each industry's special needs and requirements, the idea still has to be developed in a certain way, protected in a certain way, prepared in a certain way, and introduced in a certain way to the right people. There are ways to make that all happen and that's what this new edition is about.

If you're a new reader, I welcome you as well—and offer my genuine congratulations.

The reason for the congratulations is that I know we wouldn't be meeting here if you didn't have a fresh and original new idea, and wanted to know how to cash in on it.

You've come to the right place. This book has been published for many years in several editions and has earned the status of being the go-to source of information for folks like yourself—folks with great ideas (or who are looking for one) and who want to learn the right steps in order to be rewarded for them. Lots of people have fresh and original ideas—there's nothing novel about that—but what sets you apart is that you're taking action to make your own idea pay off for you. As Kit Carson said, referring to the pioneers' great trek westward, "The cowards won't start and the weak will die along the trail." Clearly that doesn't refer to you.

Inventors who have interesting and commercially viable new ideas or inventions find that they usually have three options. Option one is to use their original idea as the basis for starting a business. While this option clearly offers the biggest profit potential, it presents the biggest risks as well. Most folks don't take this choice, either because the idea doesn't lend itself to self-marketing or because they don't have the money or the access to money to bankroll the venture. Even if they have the money, they don't want to take the financial risk, or they don't feel they have the aptitude for being an entrepreneur. Or they may simply like their job and their lifestyle as they are and aren't interested in the kind of earth-shaking changes that entrepreneurship carries with it.

The second choice is to find an interested buyer and sell your idea outright. This might be a good choice for the person who has a need for instant cash, but it's likely to be the least profitable option. Since the purchaser can't know for sure how valuable the offering might be, the idea will be grossly undervalued to minimize the risk, and the seller will often wind up with far less than the idea is worth. The classic example is when Stanley Weston, the fellow who developed the G.I. Joe idea, sold it outright to the Hasbro Toy Company for $100,000, thinking he made a wonderful deal for himself. If he had licensed the idea instead of selling it, the thousands would have been millions.

Which brings us to the third and most popular option: licensing. The inventor gives or lends the production and marketing rights for his new invention or idea to a company in the appropriate business, which in turn pays the inventor a small percentage for every product sold. All the risk is borne by the licensee, the inventor's financial expenditure is usually modest, the interruption in the inventor's lifestyle is little more than a speed bump, and the income is passive, meaning once the deal is made, the inventor moves on to other things and the royalty checks come in automatically every month.

Since licensing is far and away the most popular option, that's what this book is dedicated to. I've been in this business for years and years, and if I can't show you what to do and how to do it, I don't know who can. Step by step, what to do first and what to do next, I will give you my secrets for what I know works—right up to the point where you leave the licensee's office with a smile on your face, a contract in your pocket, and a check in your hand. Big licensing deals are made every day by just regular folks with great ideas and who have the knowledge, grit, and determination to see it through. So what are we waiting for? Let's get started!

INTRODUCTION

*With money in your pocket, you are wise,
you are handsome, and you sing well, too.*
—Anonymous

When I wrote the first edition of this book, way back in the Dark Ages, I had to decide how to organize the information to make it as meaningful and helpful to readers as possible. I figured that by telling what I know, I'd not be creating an army of competitors; I'd be creating some new colleagues. Creating ideas for profit is a lonely business, and those of us who do it for a living are a small hardy band. The demand for fresh, innovative new product ideas, or popular new TV show ideas, or brilliant new software programs is so huge and never ending, and those of us devoted to supplying them are so few, that I can use all the help I can get!

This is an odd business to be in but one that I find exhilarating, creative, and totally satisfying. There are no seasons, no good times, and no bad times—everything depends on the quality of the idea and into whose hands it's placed. In good times companies are flush with money to spend on interesting and innovative new products, and in bad times companies need these fresh and innovative product ideas to help get them back into the black. What other business is like that? And even better—there's no competition. You can license your brilliant idea to company A, but so can I (or to company B, C, or D). No company ever said they had too many wonderful products and weren't open to hearing about another one. And the beauty of this is that there is no risk and no investment! Well, yes, there is *some* investment—but compared to the money pit you encounter when starting your own business, it's a pittance.

So anyway, with the attitude of telling all that I've learned in the decades of dreaming up and licensing ideas, I had to figure out how to do it as productively as possible without jumping all over the place and just giving a bunch of pep talks. I hate books like that. I wanted my book to have solid step-by-step nuts-and-bolts information that folks could use to their profit, not just a sales pitch for positive thinking. I decided the logical way to approach the problem is to figure out the process I go through myself, and use that as the book's structure. After all, I've dreamed up and licensed more than 100 of my own ideas, so there has to be some system to it.

Let's see, hmm—well first, obviously you have to dream up the idea—it doesn't matter if it's for a new kitchen gadget or a new software app—first comes the idea. And then, let's see, hmm—the next obvious step is to make sure it's new and original. There's no sense in wasting time on an idea that's not different or better than what's already out there. And next, hmm—if the idea truly is original, you will probably have to protect your idea in one fashion or another and then get it ready to show it to the world. Since this is a face-to-face business, next, logically, is to get an appointment with the right person at the right company. How do you prepare for that? What do you say? And finally, assuming the prospective licensee loves what you're showing him and says, "Great! Okay—what's the deal?" you can't just say, "Duh." You need to know what a licensing contract looks like and what you have a right to demand to ensure that you earn what you're entitled to.

So I put that all down in list form (I make lists of everything), and when I looked at it, an amazing discovery popped out: I had invented my own C.R.A.S.H. course in product licensing! It was so obvious, it was staring me in the face. *C* means you **Create** the idea. *R* means you **Research** the idea. *A* means you take **Action** by protecting and preparing the idea. *S* means you go out and **Sell** the idea. And *H* means you reap the **Harvest** by understanding what a licensing deal is all about to ensure that you get everything you should. Brilliant! There was no one around to pat me on the back, so I did it myself. That's one of my inventions—a self-back-patter.

This way of organizing the first two editions apparently struck a responsive chord because I've heard from countless inventors over the years who have e-mailed to my website (Money4ideas. com) to tell me how much they enjoyed the book and how much they profited from it. I can't tell you how great that makes me feel.

But why stop? This new edition, organized just like the previous editions, is, I believe, easily the best one yet. Not only does the book you have in your hands have solid information about product inventing and licensing, it also address the wider fields of new ideas for software programs, Internet business ideas, and even ideas for new reality TV shows. Ideas are ideas. Licensing is licensing. Royalties are royalties. Whatever the nature of your own idea, if it's really wonderful, there's someone who's prepared to pay you for it. My intent with this book is to make you wiser and wealthier. I know it has worked for others, and I have a good feeling that it's going to work for you as well. So let's get started. As Clint Eastwood said in *The Outlaw Josey Wales*, "Well, are you goin to pull those pistols or just stand there whistlin Dixie?"

1

CREATING THE IDEA

The Need for Need-Driven Products

*I don't care about the invention. It's the
dimes I'm after.*

—Isaac Singer

The first thing I learned long ago is that inventing is easy. I can dream up new inventions all day long. You probably can too—ideas just seem to keep popping up. However, what I also learned long ago is that, yes, inventing is easy, but the trick is to uncover what needs to be invented. That's not so easy. It doesn't matter if your idea is for a new kitchen gadget, a new software application, or a new Internet business, if you've not uncovered a need, or not found a problem demanding a solution, then success is difficult to achieve. Inventing a product that's neither wanted nor needed is not the path to success that you should embark on.

For instance, take the inventor Stanley Weston, mentioned in the Preface. As you'll recall, he's the originator of G.I. Joe. Inventing the character itself was the easy part. There was a TV show at the time called *The Lieutenant,* and he just copied that character for his own character. The real brilliance of Weston's idea—and what needed to be invented—was a doll that boys could play with. What Weston noticed that apparently no one else had was that boys like to play with dolls just as girls do, but there were no dolls made expressly for them. There were tin soldiers, but no dolls. And since you can't sell a doll to a little boy, he coined the name "action figure." Now, of course, it would be hard to find any little boy here in America who doesn't have one or more G.I. Joe action figures somewhere in his toy chest. First Weston uncovered the need—a doll that didn't look like a doll or would be called a doll (but still was a doll) for little boys to play with. That's the need to be filled. The invention part, what G.I. Joe himself looks like, was easy; any of us could have done it. First uncover the need, and then create the product. You'd be surprised how many inventors do it the other way around. They have an idea, become enamored with it, develop it, and then create imaginary scenarios where this product is just what's needed. "No home will be without it!" they exclaim. But you look at it, scratch your head, and say, "What are you supposed to do with this thing?"

It's not difficult to find products that folks might like to have to solve one or another of those pesky little problems that seem to plague all of us, if we have a mind-set to look for them. Picture yourself, about 20 years ago, sitting in an airport waiting for your plane, watching passengers going by, lugging heavy suitcases. You might have said to yourself, "This is so stupid, why doesn't someone invent little fold-up carts for these folks to use?" That's the need—something to make lugging luggage through airports easier. Inventing the cart itself was easy once the need was observed. And, of course, someone observing the same thing *did* invent and start manufacturing collapsible little luggage carts and was soon selling them as fast as they could make them.

And then, a few years later, we might again find you sitting in an airport waiting for a flight, and you might again notice passengers pulling their luggage through the aisles, only this time on collapsible metal carts—and you might again have said to yourself, "This is so stupid. Why do they need these dumb carts? Why not just put wheels on the bags themselves?" And, of course, someone did; the carts have virtually disappeared, and now it's almost impossible to find luggage that doesn't have built-in wheels. Inventing the cart was easy, as was inventing a way to put wheel on the luggage itself. You or I could have easily done that. The credit, however, goes to the person who noticed the need and did something about it.

WHEN IS AN IMPROVEMENT NOT ONE?

Through my website I offer to evaluate invention ideas from other inventors and I receive them by the boatload. Many are "improvements" on existing products, adding a new feature or two to a standard product, long in the marketplace. While these little tweaks might be fine, they represent the most difficult type of product to license. Since the so-called improved version of an existing product is not likely to attract a new company into the field, the likely licensee candidate would come from the ranks of those already in the business. But what's in it for them? They already have their own product and probably already know how to do what the inventor is proposing. Why pay out royalty dollars for something that, at best, might switch some sales from product A to product B? All retail products have a perceived value, and if the new features add to cost without adding to value, they're not worth bothering with. Yes, true, the new features might be enjoyed by consumers, but would they pay extra for them? It's likely that the prospective licensee has already made that determination and decided not. Otherwise he'd have already done it. My point is that most of these inventors are inventing what doesn't need to be invented.

I'm not suggesting that these improvements offered by the inventor aren't intelligently conceived—they may very well be—but a product's potential for sales and its potential for licensing are not the same thing; each has its own requirements. Companies exist by tweaking their product to make it a little different than the competition's; that's what their design departments do all day. However, tweaking is rarely enough for a licensing deal. The licensee might be quite interested in a fresh, new kind of product to bring in new sources of income, not a product in competition to what he's already selling. What good is that? In order to get a signature on a licensing agreement, the invention has to rise to the level of excitement, exclusivity, and profitability to perhaps make the prospective licensee say, "Wow!" as he rubs his hands together in greedy anticipation. That's not as difficult as I'm making it sound, but it is important to understand what the prospective licensee is hoping to see when you walk into his office.

"MOMMY, WHERE DO IDEAS COME FROM?"

There's a widely held misconception that creativity flourishes best in an unstructured environment. However, interviews with creative people show that their environments and work habits tend to be quite regulated. Ask some author about all he does before he starts writing; how every pencil has to be in a certain order, and how he has to be in a certain place at a certain time of day, and you'll start to think this guy is from another planet. But it's precisely this self-discipline that lets him do his job. It's his way of notifying his brain that it's time to get down to work. People who rely on the creation of new ideas as a profession have always known this. If there was no system, how could they stay in business? Systems are like the banks of a river; without them the river of creativity wanders all over the place, eventually disappearing.

In analyzing my own creativity process and breaking it down into steps—and in reading about creativity in general—I came to learn a few things. First, I learned that my system of creating ideas is the same system that has been identified and proved since classical times, so I wasn't doing anything new. Second, I learned that all of us have more creative ability than we could possibly imagine. Apparently, with all the research on the subject of creativity that has been conducted, no correlation exists between an exceptionally high IQ and creativity. Few of us are geniuses, but, lucky for us, that's not a requirement. What we need and what we can all acquire is the proper mind-set and a degree of discipline. The third thing I learned is to write everything down!

What works best for me, and just about everyone I know, is simple doodling. Nothing concentrates the mind more than putting a pencil to paper. I always have a notebook and a pen in my pocket. Always. I'm not alone; creative people have been doing that for centuries. In his diaries, Leonardo da Vinci, perhaps the most creative person in history, noted that his best ideas came while doodling, which he called "scribbling."

In truth, I confess, half the stuff I scribble in my notebooks is gibberish—I either can't understand what I wrote or I don't know why I wrote it—but the other half is what keeps me in business. It's like John Wanamaker, the famous department store founder, who once noted that he knows that half of his advertising is wasted but he doesn't know which half.

INTRODUCING THE FAMOUS REESE I.C.I.C.L.E. SYSTEM OF CREATIVITY

Here are the six steps to creativity, and if you told them to Aristotle back around 350 B.C., he'd probably say, "That old stuff? I knew that ages ago." As a mnemonic device, here's my six-step I.C.I.C.L.E method for remembering what the steps to creativity are:

I. Identify your general goal or objective. Define the general problem.

C. Concentrate on developing a solution. Fill your head with research.

I. Identify your goal again—but this time narrow it down to its most basic element.

C. Concentrate again—really hard—this time on the narrowly defined objective.

L. Let it go. Go to sleep, go to a party—let your subconscious go to work.

E. Eureka! Suddenly, seemingly out of the blue, the idea just seems to pop into your head. That's not by accident; it's because you gave your brain an assignment and it's ready to deliver the goods. There's no saying how long this might take—seconds or weeks—and there's no promise that you won't have to repeat the process, but it does work. You can take that to the bank.

You know how you meet someone you know on the street, chat for a moment, then each of you goes his own way—and for the life of you, you can't think of his name? And you think, and you think as hard as you can, but it just doesn't come. Chester? Charles? Something beginning with a C, you're sure, but your mind draws a blank. And then, hours later, while in the middle of taking your tango dance lesson, suddenly it pops into your head. Frank! Good old Frank! How could you forget? And suddenly you remember everything about Frank that you ever knew, and maybe some things you wish you didn't. That's just the I.C.I.C.L.E process at work. You identified the problem in the most basic way ("What's that guy's name?"), concentrated on it as hard as you could, let your subconscious do its work, and suddenly your wonderful brain delivered the goods.

Brilliant ideas don't pop into your head by accident.

THIS IS A TEST

Just now, while I'm writing this, for the fun of it, I decided to give myself a little test.

    I. I identified my problem: To come up with an Internet business for myself.

C. I concentrated on that goal, thinking about other Internet businesses I'm familiar with.

I. I decided I don't want a business that involves investing in inventory, so it has to be some sort of service business. That's my narrow objective: an Internet business with no inventory investment. And so I concentrated again, now on the narrow objective.

C.L.E. All three of these steps happened in a jumble. I thought about what kind of service business might interest me that lends itself to the Internet, and the idea for one immediately popped into my head. All of this took less than a minute—but it could have taken an hour or a week—that's not the point. The point is that it's a process, and when you're conscious that it is a process and you apply it, it does produce results.

The Internet business my little test produced is to offer hand-painted portraits in oil of children, loved ones, pets, the purchaser himself, or the dearly departed. All the customer needs to do is send me a photo of the subject and his or her credit card information. Half of the cost would be charged upon acceptance of the assignment and the other half after the customer saw a photo of the finished portrait and gives an approval.

As I discuss later in this book, in order to license an Internet business, there has to be something unique about it to give the licensee an advantage. The unique advantage that I would give to my licensee is my personal connection to some talented artists in China who can turn out beautiful portraits and who work at much lower rates than here in the United States. I'd submit the customer's photo to one of my artist friends who'd do the portrait. When the portrait was complete I'd post a picture of it on a website for the customer to visit and give his approval. The portrait would be shipped to the customer, the artist would be paid for his work, and I'd add my profit and charge the customer's credit card. Simple! The only investment would be in creating and promoting the website. Since I'm an artist, I tend to think in those directions, but so what? All of us have talents and interests that might push in one direction or another. You might be an avid fisherman and so your Internet business idea might involve fishing products. If you involve yourself in a field that you like, success is a lot easier to achieve.

Now, perhaps when I do the numbers I'll find that my portrait idea is not such a great idea after all—but I have the confidence that if I repeat the process, I can come up with something else—and that might be just what I'm looking for. But I'm no smarter than you are.

If I can do it, I'm sure you can too. It all has to do with the process. If you want to start an Internet business, you can; I'm sure of it. Let me know when you've done it; maybe I'll become a customer.

This thinking process works for anything. Suppose you, like many of us, watch reality TV shows and think, "This program is so stupid. I know I could come up with something better." The TV networks love reality shows because they're cheaper to make than dramas and some of them rack up huge audiences. So if you have a brilliant idea for a new show, why not give it a shot? Maybe you'll be a hero to one of these networks.

So, again, let's follow the process:

I. You've identified the general objective: to create a new reality show.

C. Next you're going to concentrate on this general objective by researching all the different kinds of reality shows there are. Let's see, there are documentary shows that show real people doing their jobs, such as cops arresting people; there are all sorts of dating reality shows that match prospective mates; there are hidden camera shows where people do dumb things; there are adventure shows where men and women are placed in exotic jungle locations; there are singing and dancing talent shows; there are contests where professional cooks or dress designers compete—and on and on.

It's your job to look at all these types of shows to determine what makes them tick and then to select a category that you want to focus on.

I. Let's say you've identified talent as your category. That's the narrow goal that you've decided to focus on—talented people competing against one another.

C. Now that you have identified your narrow objective, a reality show involving talented people competing against one another, it's time to focus again. Let's see: singing has been done and dancing has been done and cooking has been done and baking has been done and dress designing has been done and hair designing has been done—what's left? You think and think as hard as you can until you just can think any more. Bummer! Everything's been taken!

L. To heck with it, you let it go. You and your pals go out to the movies.

E. You're sitting in the darkened theater; the movie is half over, and the hero is chained to the table and the buzz saw is getting closer and closer—and suddenly, eureka! Country music! Nobody has done country music! Suppose you have a group of country music writers and every week they're given a scenario ("My boyfriend's in jail and his cute buddy keeps coming over") and they have to write and sing a song that fits. The judges are famous country and western stars. The person who writes and sings the worst song goes home and the final winner gets a Nashville appearance, a recording contract, money, and so on. Wow! "Excuse me guys, I gotta go!" You jump out of your seat to rush home to fill in the details. It's the I.C.I.C.L.E. system—it never lets you down.

Give your brain a rest for the eureka moment.

INSIDE JOBS, HEAD STARTS, LEG UPS, AND STUFF LIKE THAT

Perhaps you already have worked out your new invention, but if not, then I should tell you that it has been my experience that the most successful inventors are those who invent products for industries in which they're already professionally involved. Since we know that the trick in this business is to invent what needs to be invented, it's easy to see why those folks have a clear head start or a leg up over the rest of us. By virtue of their personal industry involvement and experience, they can see opportunities that probably would elude the rest of us. They know what's been done and tried and what the industry is looking for, and they can therefore invent to that goal. It's very hard for an inventor to simply pop into an unknown industry with a product idea that's so refreshingly new that it'll be greeted with enthusiasm by those who have spent entire careers in the business. Yes, that does sometimes happen, but much more often the proposed product turns out to be something that already exists, or has been tried in the past, or has long been known to industry insiders.

So if you're just starting out—first, please, start within your own profession. A chef is more likely to come up with a great new kitchen gadget than an accountant who likes to dabble in the kitchen once in a while. If you're searching for a great new software idea, you're much more likely to find one that can help you and your professional colleagues than those in some other industry.

I don't mean that it's impossible to create profitable ideas for inventions or businesses or software programs outside of your professional life—only that it's a more difficult route. However, certainly other opportunities exist. Other than the work environment, the logical places to look for new invention opportunities are in familiar areas like home, or in familiar activities like your hobbies. Just as pearls come from irritated oysters, product ideas can often come from common, daily annoyances. Mommies with new infants are famous for dreaming up ideas for baby-care products. Taking care of a baby is so time consuming and on occasion so exasperating, that any product that makes it easier can be a welcome one. There are even some Internet companies dedicated to marketing mommy ideas. Anything that's an irritation to you might be an irritation to millions of others—and that's how simple but great ideas are born.

Take this simple irritation: trying to hold a leaf bag open when your hands are full. This irritation happens all the time since one hand must hold the rake and the other hand holds the leaves to the rake. Someone I know, many years ago, came up with a simple metal bag frame to keep the leaf bag open, and now everyone sells them. That's not some brilliant cancer-curing invention, but most of us aren't in the cancer-curing business. All we need is a simple idea that performs a function perceived as useful enough that a person would buy one.

I know a mother in Texas who became exasperated with using poster board to help her child with school projects. She mentioned it to her sister, and together they invented "Ghost Lines," a barely visible printed grid on poster board that helps a person print or cut in straight lines. They licensed the idea to one of the major paper companies and now I see their product wherever poster board is sold.

"Hey! Why didn't someone think of that before?" Those are the words successful inventors long to hear. Einstein, the genius, once said that he had only one original idea in his career, and it was just a theory at that. Maybe one great idea is all you need—but if you exploit it properly, it could change your life.

CAVEATS, WARNINGS, CAUTIONS, AND PLACES NOT TO GO

The last thing I want to do is discourage you. I want you to invent whatever you care to, be it a new product, a new software application, or whatever—I'm behind you 110 percent.

You can count on me. However, I feel duty-bound to mention a few categories of product that are extremely difficult to license—not impossible, but really, really hard. All things being equal, I'd rather see you focus your talents in other directions.

The first category I'd like to see you avoid is board games. I know they're fun to create for lots of clever folks, men and women alike, but the world just doesn't need all the cute, clever, and perfectly intelligent games that these folks can produce. If you count yourself among that group, I'm sorry, but those are the facts. Electronic games have so taken over the industry that the traditional type of board game is barely holding on by its fingertips.

The days when the family sat around the dining room table in the evening and played one of these nice board games is a memory, something that Norman Rockwell might have painted. One game executive is quoted as remarking that even Monopoly, if it was introduced today, would have a tough time finding a company to produce it.

The hard truth is most of the major game companies won't even look at a board game idea from an outside source unless it has a famous name or popular TV show or movie attached to it. These companies have the staff to make all the generic board games they need themselves, without paying royalties to anyone. Licensing is rare, but even when it does occur, it's usually for a game that is being self-marketed by the inventor and exhibits a proven consumer audience. Scrabble is a perfect example. For a number of years in the 1940s, a married couple from Connecticut, the Brunots, having been turned down by all the game companies, manufactured the game in their living room, selling a few thousand sets every year. By pure chance, in 1952, the owner of Macy's happened to play the game while on vacation and ordered it placed into all of Macy's toy departments. Macy's promoted the game, sales took off, and then, of course, all the game companies that previously turned it down were now happy to sign a licensing deal. Finally the licensing rights wound up with Mattel, and the game continues to be one of the world's bestsellers. If you insist on being a game inventor, your best chance are young children's games if they have a physical component that involves a little skill or dexterity, or a party game with some kind of physical fun or harmless sexual component. Those are a bit easier to license.

Statistics say there are more than 26 million golfers in the United States. You can double that, I suppose, if you include the rest of the world. If there are 50 million in total, my guess is that 40 million of them have invented a golf product to make a player's game better or easier. Okay, a slight exaggeration—but so many golfers have invented so many new training techniques or tools or devices or gadgets to make the stroll around the course easier or to turn that poor duffer into an amazing player with drives straight and true and putts that never miss, that I sort of groan when an inventor sends me a new one. I don't mean that these are stupid ideas—lots of them perhaps have merit—but there are so many golf inventions floating around, with the patent office files bulging, that finding a licensing partner is really, really difficult. If you're a golfer reading this—tell the truth—in the back of your head you have a fantastic new golf product idea that you're a preparing to spring on the world. Right? Okay, maybe your idea really is what everyone has been waiting for. I hope so—but don't say you weren't warned.

Another category that I suggest you avoid is products that depend on a license for their consumer interest. If you have an idea, say, for a pen desk set shaped like a car that has NASCAR printed on it, and if it would just be an ordinary desk set without the logo, then, my friend, you'll have a tough row to hoe while looking for a licensee. First, you can't license what you don't own (the NASCAR license) and you can't guarantee the desk set manufacturer would get a license even if he applied. And even if the desk set manufacturer did get the license, he'd then presumably be obligated to pay out two royalties—one to NASCAR and one to you for the suggestion. That's not likely to happen.

The exception is if the invented product does have merit on its own and that the addition of a popular licensed logo or character might make it even better. That has happened to me. I licensed a special kind of bedtime dolls to a bedding manufacture and they decided to fashion these dolls as licensed characters instead of the generic ones I had designed. I had to agree to reduce my royalties in half to partially compensate them for the other licensing fees, and I did so on the premise that sales would more than double in this manner. However, the fact that my product could be (and was) licensed on its own merits is what made that deal possible.

And finally, if I were king, I'd decree that you not look for a licensee based on your exclamation that you have the next Pet Rock! The bankruptcy graveyard is filled with companies and individuals who think they have the next Pet Rock. I personally am a real sucker for nutty fad items, and I have created more than my share. I'm the guy who invented inflatable furniture, and I'm the guy who invented those reindeer antlers that folks put on their dogs every Christmas (among other nutty items that I'm too embarrassed to mention). However, I know how hard it is to license stuff like that.

The problem is that nobody knows for sure what item is suddenly going to take off and become a big national seller. And even when items do, the manufacturer is usually just as amazed as everyone else. I've made a study of fad items, trying to discover if there is a common thread among the winners that could be duplicated—and there isn't. There just doesn't seem to be any rhyme or reason to it— hit fad items have a life of their own, and they are the right product at precisely the right time. Since there is no predictability, companies are reluctant to take on the legal and financial obligations of a licensing agreement just to find out. The failures are so many and the successes so few, that it's not a risk most companies are willing to take. They might do it for a product they've developed themselves, figuring that one hit can make up for lots of losers, but taking on the costs and obligations of a licensing agreement is a whole different matter. Again, as with board games and golf items, licensing is not impossible, just difficult.

"A DREAM IS A WISH YOUR HEART MAKES" (BUT YOU CAN'T LICENSE IT)

I've come to realize that when folks complain about "their idea" being marketed by someone else, they don't mean that someone crept into their workshop to steal the secret plans that they toiled over; they just mean that one time they had a dream, an idle notion, that there should be a product to do something or other, and one day saw something similar in a store. No one beat them to it; they were never in the race.

First of all, an inventor should have an understanding of what the licensee is willing to pay for. If the licensee is a manufacturer, every day he or she arises and thinks about his or her arch competitor. "What's that lousy bum doing? What rotten plans is that jerk hatching to get me pushed out of my biggest customers?" The competitor is doing the same thing—it's a battle that never ends. If you, as an inventor, come along with a new weapon to give one of these warriors an edge, presumably in the form of a terrific new product invention, you'll be rewarded with cash advances and royalties. However, this prospective licensee expects you to put a fully developed and proven product in his hands, not just some suggestion for one. He wants to receive a shining new sword to go out and do battle with, not a lump of steel and a pencil sketch. It is the fully fashioned sword itself, a kind of sword that has never been seen before, that might earn the rewards, not simply the suggestion for one.

An inventor sent me an idea. "Hey Harvey, I have this great idea for a new toy! It's a teddy bear with green fur I call Flippo. When you squeeze Flippo's paw, he jumps in the air, does a double flip, lands on his behind and sings 'God Bless America.'"

"Wow!" I say, "How does it work?"

"I told you," comes the exasperated reply, "you squeeze his paw."

Okay, I confess, I made that up, but it's not far from the truth. Here's another example that is true. There's a popular, common household product that comes in 6-oz. and 12-oz. sizes. The inventor believed that sales for this product would greatly increase if it was also made it in a 2-oz. travel size. She wanted me to make the suggestion to the company and arrange for her to receive a royalty on every 2-oz. package they sold. This inventor is not stupid—the 2-oz. suggestion might be perfectly sensible—but folks like this, or the person with the flipping teddy bear, just don't understand what has to be placed on a manufacturer's desk in order to make him reach for his checkbook.

Whether you have a software idea that you want someone to license, or a reality show idea, or an Internet business idea, or an idea for a new gardening tool, you have to deliver the goods. Companies license inventions or fully formed and proven concepts, not simply observations that a product to do a certain thing or a piece of software to accomplish a certain result might be popular. As they say, the devil is in the details.

So, now that you've thought up your brilliant idea, what's next? An author named E. L. Simpson once said, "Getting an idea should be like sitting on a tack. It should make you jump up and do something," which is just what we're going to do in the next chapter.

2

How to Research and Evaluate Your New Idea

It's time to stand up and cheer for the doer, the achiever—the one who recognizes the challenge and does something about it.
—Vince Lombardi, Coach of the Green Bay Packers

So far, all you've spent on your idea is some time and maybe a few dollars for this book (unless you're reading it in the library). You have an idea in your head and maybe some doodles on a scrap of paper. You can walk away and no harm done. However, we will soon be approaching the point where some money must be spent—maybe some serious money—so we want to tread carefully.

The next step in the process, thankfully a free or nominally free one, is to search the market to determine whether your idea has enough originality and commercial potential to continue with its development. Depending on what you find, you'll either walk away or start reaching for your checkbook. So honesty, as they say, is the best policy.

Alfred Hitchcock, the great film director, used to say that the crime the evildoers commit in his movies—stealing the famous diamond or the secret plans or anything else—was incidental. It was, as he called it, simply the McGuffin—a device to move the story along. The story was really about the chase, the danger, and the boy-meets-girl love connection. I urge you to regard your idea the same way—it's a McGuffin—simply a commercial idea to hopefully earn you some money. It's not "your baby" that no one dare speak evil of (or assuming that they're idiots if they do). If some company tells me (politely) that they think my idea stinks, they don't mean that I stink and I don't take it personally; it's just business. McGuffins come and go—if one of them turns out to not be as great as you thought, so what? You can think up another one. I have a drawer full of McGuffins that never went anywhere, but they're ancient history—I've moved on—with more new McGuffins in my head than I know what to do with.

The standards to objectively evaluate your idea depend upon the idea itself. What factors might sway a manufacturer of pet toys are not the same as what might sway a TV network executive or someone looking to invest money in a new Internet business or a company deciding whether to distribute your new software program—and so we'll look at them independently. The bar is obviously higher for some than for others.

RESEARCHING YOUR NEW PRODUCT IDEA

What your objective at this point should be is to determine whether you really have a good idea for a product and, if so, to see if it has already been done. Your mother or your wife or husband or friends might all tell you the idea is brilliant, but what do they know? They love you; they're not going to tell you your idea is stupid. And don't ask your patent attorney. His advice about the marketability of your idea is of little value. Not only is he not an expert on product marketing, but he's in the patent business—he's not going to drive a potential customer away by telling him he thinks the idea is no good. He's not stupid. It's the truth you're after—and you have to be able to handle it. It's better to be disappointed now than to learn the truth about your idea further down the road after you've poured your heart and soul (and money) into it.

The best truth-teller you're liable to find is someone with experience in this business and with no vested interest in your success. There are professionals in whatever industry your product belongs, and you should be able to engage one or another in a conversation about your idea without getting into the specifics of the idea itself. For instance, if you had an idea for an automotive after-market product, you might stroll into the local automotive store and tell the clerk that you're looking for a product to do such-and-such (close to what your own idea is). The clerk might put precisely that product into your hands. Bummer! Or the clerk might say, "Y'know, we get calls for that kind of product a lot. I don't know why someone doesn't make it." Or he might say, "No, we don't have a product like that, but here's something better." Whether the news is good or bad, when you leave the store you'll know a lot more about the value and originality of your idea than before you entered.

The last kind of entity to seek advice from are those invention submission companies that advertise on TV. They will offer to evaluate your idea "for free" and will absolutely, positively, without a shadow of a doubt report back that your idea is brilliant and that they rarely have ever met a creative genius of your caliber. With them at your side, you will conquer the world! And then, of course, they will proceed to sell you one "must-have" service after another, promising that each step is bringing you closer and closer to the promised land. First, they'll tell you they need to do some market research (for which you'll pay, maybe $1,000). And then they'll tell you they need to do some patent research (another $1,000 or so). And then they'll tell you that you *must* get a patent (many thousands more), and then they'll tell you they need to prepare a presentation for your product to show to companies waiting to see it (more thousands), and on and on and on, until they've gotten all they can—at which point they'll drop you by the roadside, sadder and poorer. A lot poorer.

The UIA is trade group for independent inventors. Here's a list of "Red Flag Warnings" they published to serve as a warning guide for inventors to avoid invention promotion companies that engage in the following tactics:

1. Company refuses to provide in writing the number of ideas they have represented and how many inventors made more money than they invested.

2. Company refuses to provide in writing the number of ideas that have been sent to them and how many they accepted.

3. Company refuses to provide to the inventor at least three clients (preferably in the inventor's home area) who can verify the company's credibility.

4. Salesperson applies pressure to send money right away.

5. Company tells you to fully describe your idea in writing and then tells you to mail this information to yourself and not open the envelope. This ploy is used to give the inventor the false impression that the idea is somehow protected. In fact, it does absolutely nothing.

6. Company recommends that a design patent be applied for (which is usually valueless).

7. Company provides a patent search without patentability opinion.

8. Salesperson can never be reached directly without leaving a message. Typically, the salesperson is actually working out of his home, using a phone drop.

9. Company claims to be located in one state, but all correspondence is postmarked from another state. These companies commonly use fictitious addresses and mail drops to hide their actual location.

10. Company runs slick ads on radio, TV, and in magazines.

11. Company offers money-back guarantee if patent not issued (they can always get a patent on something).

If there's an invention company you're thinking of using, and if you're not sure these Red Flag Warnings apply, there are a couple of reliable way to check them out.

1. The U.S. Patent and Trademark office publishes complaints filed by private inventors about certain companies. You can check to see if the company you're preparing to use is on the

list and what others are saying about them (www.uspto.gov/ inventors/scam_prevention/complaints/index.jsp).

2. A patent attorney friend of mine, Michael Neustel, runs a very popular website naming marketing companies identified with unscrupulous practices (www.InventorFraud.com) and also identifies what he calls "The Good Guys" in this business.

3. Another friend, Ronald J. Riley, runs a website (www.inventored .org), where he passionately calls out these unsavory invention promoters, naming them by name.

Any company that offers a "free evaluation" does so with a self-serving reason, so be warned. How reliable can this "free evaluation" of your idea be when the company offering it uses it as a basis to sell you their other services? How dumb do they think you are? However, there's good news. There are organizations that will charge you for a product evaluation (usually around $200) and that have nothing to sell you. They can therefore be relied upon to provide an honest, impartial, intelligent evaluation of your new product idea, along with suggestions and recommendations. Most (except me) are governmental, university, or organizationally connected. Here's a partial list:

Wisconsin Innovation Service Center: www.uww.edu

I2 Innovation Institute: www.wini2.com

United Inventors Association: www.uiausa.org

Canadian Innovation Centre: www.Innovationcentre.ca

Harvey Reese Associates: www.money4ideas.com

Determining the commercial value of your idea is subjective, even from the experts, but true honesty in interpreting what you learn will go far in properly assessing your idea's commercial value. Unfortunately, many inventors, enamored with their ideas, hear only what they want to. When inventors send me their ideas, part of the evaluation we do includes two worksheets: one addressing the idea from the point of view of self-marketing, the other, from product licensing. Here are 20 questions from the licensing worksheet that we grade from unknown or not applicable, to low, average, high, and very high. You can informally grade yourself as you view the questions. Since your answers will unavoidably be subjective, I'm not suggesting this as a reliable test—only as a way to prompt you to think about the issues. Any prospective licensee will automatically ask and answer these questions in his or her mind, and they will certainly influence any decision.

PRODUCT EVALUATION WORKSHEET

Very High   High   Low   Unknown

1. Degree to which this is a fully developed, proven idea. _____

2. Probability that the product will do what's claimed for it. _____

3. Probability that industry companies will view this product as new and novel. _____

4. Probability that the product is addressing issues that the industry has been unable to solve. _____

5. Probability that this product has either been done before or has been considered and rejected by company management. _____

6. Probability that this product would be immediately recognizable as being superior in function or benefit over existing products. _____

7. Probability for this product to create new profit opportunities for the licensee rather than switching sales from already existing products in his line. _____

8. Level of exclusivity (patent protection) that this product can offer to a prospective licensee. _____

9. Regarding this product, level of importance of patent protection to a prospective licensee. _____

10. Probability for this product to achieve a level of sales success to pique the interest of a prospective licensee. _____

11. Level and quality of existing competition affecting market entry. _____

12. Degree of financial investment required in relation to potential payoff. _____

13. Degree that product safety issues would affect prospective licensee's decision. _____

14. Degree to which this product meets current trends. _____

15. Degree of ease by which product's advantages are immediately recognized by consumers. _____

16. Degree to which this product can be sold through regular retail channels rather than through special marketing efforts. _____

17. Degree of probable retailer resistance based on competitive situation, difficulty to display, low profit potential, or any other adverse market factors. _____

18. Probability for this product to open new distribution opportunities for licensee. _____

19. Probability for this product to be the genesis for a full product line versus being a one shot, short-term product. _____

20. Level to which success for this product is dependent upon the licensing of a famous character, logo, athletic endorsement, or sport league affiliation. _____

As we already discussed, if your idea is just a tweaking of an existing product, it will probably be hard to license. If your idea is for a board game, or a golf idea, or a fad product, it would similarly be difficult to license. As we also discussed, asking whether a product will sell is not the same question as whether it can be licensed. In a big, rich country like ours, lots of products can find an audience—but in order to find a licensee, your product idea needs a level of excitement, novelty, exclusivity, and profit potential to make the prospect sit up and take notice. In determining whether to license an idea, there are a few other considerations. For instance:

Small Products Produce Small Results

That headline doesn't mean small size; it means small profits. Some product ideas, even though they might be perfectly sensible, simply don't have the potential to get anyone excited. The hard truth is that even under the best of circumstances, companies instinctively hate to sign licensing contracts. They don't like the constrictions that a licensing agreement places on them, and they hate paying royalties to outsiders. They'll go for a licensing deal (kicking and screaming), only if the idea seems to present itself as an opportunity too good to let pass by. Not every offered product will strike them in that manner—not because there's anything wrong with the idea, but because it just doesn't strike them as anything worth bothering with.

Some years ago a friend of mine came up with a new design for a picture hanger. It wasn't the most brilliant product I ever saw, but it was certainly okay. He asked if I could get it licensed, and because he was a friend I said I'd try—knowing in my heart I'd not be successful.

I showed the design to a half dozen companies that sell picture hangers as part of their line and all said the same thing; the idea was nice, but it didn't matter. I knew what they meant; it's what I expected them to say. Typically, companies that sell picture hangers sell whole lines of gadgets, of which the picture hanger is just one item. A retailer will buy the line from one company or another because their prices are better or because their quality is better or their packaging is better—or simply because the like the salesperson better. None of these retailers buy the line because one company has a better picture hanger—it's just another item on a peg and customers will buy what they see. The picture hangers these companies already sell do the job, and so my friend's improved product is not going to affect anyone's sales and profits, so why bother?

I don't mean that the retailer doesn't want to sell the best product—but often the quality being maybe a notch higher just doesn't matter. Every product can possibly be a little better, but where does it end? You have to take a cold look at your own product to see if it's another picture hanger. If it is, this is the time to find out. It's not that the consumer wouldn't like the improved picture hanger, but the consumer is not our customer. Our customer is the company that makes the product to sell to the consumer. If the company doesn't benefit, there's no deal.

I don't mean to suggest that simple ideas aren't licensable—because many are. The reason no one wanted my friend's picture hanger is not because it was a simple product, but because it was just a bit better than what they're already selling, and the realities of the marketplace gave it little licensable value. However, I assure you, lots of simple ideas get licensed every day. Often simple ideas, if they're for original products and not just duplicates of existing ones, are the easiest to license because they're easy to understand, easy to make, and can enjoy a quick easy sale. If it wasn't for simple ideas, I'd have long ago been out of business. I'm the king of simple ideas.

Long ago I owned a manufacturing company with lots of employees and lots of machinery, but I didn't enjoy being in a factory every day and happily gave it up. Deciding what to do next, I took inventory of my strengths and realized that what I could do best was create products. And so I figured—why should I spend time doing what I hate to do? There are guys who love running factories. I'll give them my new product ideas—let them have the responsibilities to produce and sell them—and they'll just pay me a little bit on each sale they make. They're happy and I'm happy. As far as I know, this is a business I made up for myself; and I've been doing it ever since.

My first target customer was a small giftware company located nearby. Even then I knew that this was a face-to-face business and so I needed to work with a company that was easy to get to. This company's principal business was importing artificial roses made of dyed wood shavings that looked and felt like the real thing. Knowing I had to dream up something to compliment what they were already doing, my invention was one of their roses, attached to a floral greeting card with a ribbon added, packed in a see-through gift box that said something like "A Valentine Rose for my Sweetheart (Wife, Mother, etc.)."

I'm not bragging about the brilliance of this idea—I know it was dumber than dumb—but it was a product that the owner of the company knew he could sell, and so it had value.

Actually, it went on to sell for a number of years. My point is this: Don't dismiss simple ideas just because they're simple. If the idea is new, not done before, and if the company recognizes it as something that will sell and that fits into their product line, they will happily reward you with royalties for bringing it to them. Why not? These people aren't stupid.

My dumb little product met all the requirements for a licensing deal—it had the look of being salable, the investment was modest, and it complemented the product line that the company was already selling instead of competing with it. In other words, it provided the company with an easy new source of income rather than just switching some sales from their own product A to my product B.

Fashion Items Don't Make the Cut

The problem with finding a licensing partner for a fashion item is that this is such a notorious knockoff business that there's little that you could supply to your prospective licensee that her competitors can't (and won't) knock off virtually overnight. The model hasn't even left the runway at the fashion show before the knockoff process begins. Fashion items are commonly known as cut-and-sew products—meaning no investment in tooling and no investment in equipment. The fashion house doesn't produce the garment or accessory product bearing its label—that's done in some third-world country that has at least enough power to run some sewing machines. Because entry is so fast and cheap, companies can instantly copy anything that's hot. Patents are expensive to obtain and horribly expensive to defend, and since fashion items typically come and go quite fast, it's moot anyway. That's why famous designers can license their famous names, but make no effort to license their specific designs. Clothing fashion ideas are so difficult to license that it's almost just not worth the effort to try. If you're a fashionista inventor—sorry, but better to find out now.

RESEARCHING YOUR NEW PRODUCT INVENTION

The U.S. Patent and Trademark Office, which has patents on file dating all the way back to the founding of the country, is a good place to start your research. The Patent Office has gone out of its way to make their website (www.uspto.gov) as user-friendly as possible, so that's a logical jumping-off point. If your idea is simple, you can probably conduct the search yourself; it's not that difficult. If you're not confident that you can do a thorough search on your own, the Patent and Trademark Office maintains one or more patent depositories in a public or university library in every state, which you can visit. These depositories have the same information that you can get online, but they have trained personnel to guide and assist you. A list of their locations is in the Appendix.

If your idea is complicated, complex, or technical you might want to hire a professional search company. Most of these professional searchers are former patent examiners, so they can probably do a better job faster and more thoroughly than most of us could possibly do on our own, and their interpretation of what they find will probably be more reliable. Using professional searchers is not cheap and probably not necessary for simple, everyday products. However, for a complex, technical invention, what these professional searchers find or don't find, and how they interpret the results, may turn out to be money well spent. Here's the contact information for some of them; there are plenty more.

EnvisionIP: www.Envision.com

Patex Research and Consulting: www.Patex.com

Patent Complete: www.PatentComplete.com

SearchQuest: www.SearchQuestPatents.com

LegalZoom: www.LegalZoom.com

There are also independent websites, other than the patent office site, where you can conduct a patent search on your own. While the Patent Office does make every effort to provide an accessible website, it is still the government, so even "easy" is complicated. www.Google.com/patents and www.FreePatentsonLine.com are the ones I usually use myself because they can give me the same information faster and easier.

However, before poring over patents, a Google.com or Bing.com search can be fast and thorough and most often makes a patent search unnecessary. If the product you describe exists anywhere in the world, or has been patented here in the United States, it will probably show up if you do a determined search. The trick is to find the right search term to produce the right results. Sometimes it takes several stabs at a definition to request the precise information you're seeking, but usually one search leads to the other and you'll get what you're looking for. Just stay with it until you're confident that you've exhausted the possibilities. An inventor sent me an idea for a product recently that I was confident existed—I thought I might have even seen one—but trying to get it come up on a Google search was proving to be a problem. I tried one search term after another, producing no results. If I wasn't so confident that I had already seen this product, I might have quit at that point. However, I stuck with it and finally, on what I guess was about the eighth turn of a phrase, I found the right search words to give me what I was looking for. And bingo! There was the twin of the inventor's product already in the marketplace, as I thought.

Of all the inventions and product ideas that inventors submit to me (and I see lots of them), I would guess that at least half have already been done or there's a reason why they haven't (harmful, illegal, etc.). I can usually find this information so quickly (and not because I'm a Google search genius) that I have to wonder why the inventor sent me the idea in the first place. He could have done the search himself in a New York minute and uncovered the same information. I can only assume, as earlier suggested, that many inventors simply don't want to know—or they are so convinced of their product idea's brilliance and originality that they think a search isn't necessary. They will say that they looked in stores and didn't see it, I assume feeling they did all the searching that's necessary. But looking in stores is just scratching the surface.

I'm not exaggerating when I say that at least half of the invention ideas I see are quickly and easily determined to be not original. Often I can just look at the drawing or photo of the inventor's idea and say, "This idea is just so obvious, it *has* to exist" (or there's a good reason why it doesn't), and in a jiffy I can find out I'm right. It's frankly just common sense, and I have to wonder what in the world the inventor was thinking. I assure you, if you don't do this search yourself, you can be sure that any prospective licensee who has any interest in your idea will do so, and if there's bad news to learn, it's better to find it now rather than thousands of dollars later.

One time I had a really funny idea—a dog collar with a recording device on it that could operate by a remote control in the pet owner's pocket. The device would be prerecorded with all sorts of flirty things, so when a pretty girl walked by, the "dog" would have some smart aleck remark to make. But hey, it was the dog. Who can blame a dog? I took the idea to a company I know, and they were so excited that we did the deal on the spot (I never make a call without a contract in my pocket). The president even called home to tell his wife what an amazing product idea just walked in the door.

A week later I had an e-mail from the president; "Go to this site (xxxx.com), then call me."

In doing their due diligence, the company uncovered some small company in some place like North Snowshoe, Canada, that was selling the same thing. What an embarrassment! I did a search, but the company did a better one. Of course, all moneys had to be refunded and the product filed away in the losers' drawer. If this product idea had been dreamed up internally by a salaried employee, the company might have proceeded anyway—but a product from an outsider, expecting the company to take on the legal and financial responsibilities of a licensing agreement, has a higher level of standards to meet.

So, between the patent office website, Internet searches, visits to stores, and looking through catalogs, make as sure as is humanly possible that your idea is truly original. Remember, so far you haven't spent any money. Search well and maybe you won't have to.

Make sure your invention is original.

RESEARCHING YOUR TV GAME SHOW OR REALITY SHOW IDEA

Researching your idea's originality is the easy part—the hard part comes later when you have to put it all together and get a pitch meeting. We'll get to that later; for now you just want to be assured that the essential idea has enough that's new and original about it to move on with its development. It's doubtful that you have a wholly new idea—nobody does—but your idea has to be original enough so that the networks can't feel they've already done it. *Jeopardy*, for instance, is just another question and answer show—but what makes it original is that Merv Griffin, the fellow who created it, had the brilliant idea for the host to give the answer and for the contestants to race against each other to think up the right question.

Google Directory has an extensive list of TV reality shows and game shows, most of which you probably never heard of. Yahoo! Directory has similar lists, as does Wikipedia, among other sites. Take your time, look through the appropriate lists carefully—if you don't find your own idea or any that is dangerously close, then it's probably safe to move to the next step. The only other thing is to determine if the essential idea has broad enough potential appeal for any TV network to want to produce it. You might have a great idea for a show about a bunch of CPAs competing to see who can balance a ledger fastest—but who would watch?

RESEARCHING A NEW SOFTWARE PROGRAM

The development of a new software program requires such a large investment, even for a demonstration prototype, that a great deal of honest, non-deluding research should be done before proceeding. The questions to ask are easy; the answers may not be so easy. Is there a genuine demand for this new program? How many customers might there be? What might they be willing to pay for it? Are these customers easily identifiable and easily reached? Do other competitive software programs exist? How is yours superior? How will it compete? Where will it be sold?

It's possible to find a licensee who will reward you simply for the suggestion of a program, but that's quite difficult. In software, the value is in the doing, at least to the extent of having a prototype to show the look of the program and how it works. You might then have a better chance of licensing it as is—or perhaps the company will pay you to complete the development. The easiest to license is a wholly developed program that you can put into the licensee's hands—but since considerable development costs might be involved, you might need partners for the financing. If that's the case, it's not enough to convince yourself of the idea's validity; you need the facts and figures to convince others as well. How do you know how large the potential market is? Are there some statistics to back up your estimate? How do you know what these customers might pay? Do you have a record of what similar programs charge? How would the licensee reach the potential customers? How are competitive products distributed? Anyone being asked to invest money in the program will ask questions like this, and you have to be prepared with the answers. Hunches and seat-of-the pants guesswork might be fine for developing a little toy or gadget where the risks are minuscule, but software is the big leagues and requires big-league thinking.

You should also visit Internet sites such as www.thesoftwarenetwork .com,which lists many software manufacturers and the types of software programs they sell. If any seem to be marketing programs that are close to what you have in mind, a visit to their website will give you the specifics. None of the company lists on these individual websites is exhaustive, but if you visit several—like www.altiusdirectory .com/Computers/ or www.programplaz.com—you'll gain a good sense of what's available. One of these websites pretty much leads to another with a simple Google search. This is a huge industry, so the research isn't done in a moment—but since the time and money involved in writing a software program is substantial, proceeding without doing your homework would not be wise.

RESEARCHING A NEW INTERNET BUSINESS IDEA

The good thing about the Internet is that it's cheap and easy to set up a website and be in business almost overnight. No one knows if you're some big company or if you're working in your pajamas out of a small efficiency apartment. The bad thing about the Internet is that it's cheap and easy to set up a website and be in business almost overnight. No one knows if you're some big company or if you're working in your pajamas out of a small efficiency apartment.

The fact that entry is simple and cheap might be a good thing if you're planning to set up a little sideline Internet business for yourself—but it's not a good thing if you hope to license your Internet business idea to another entity. It's not enough to just be able to prove that your business idea has huge potential—lots of Internet businesses can make that claim. In order to get the attention of a potential licensee, you need to have something unique and proprietary that would separate your web business from all of the copycat companies sure to follow. Nobody, not even your rich Uncle Louie, is going to pay you money for something that will have a gazillion imitators almost overnight. You need to give Uncle Louie some kind of edge, something that's his alone to let him stand out from the crowd. Uncle Louie might be ugly, but he's not a dope.

Some years back a fellow named Jim McCann captured the phone number 1-800-Flowers and the web address www.Flowers.com, and that put him in business. His pansies probably aren't any better than the next guy's, but what a powerful edge he has with his phone number and web address! If you want to send flowers to your friend in the hospital in Sheboygan, what are the chances that you'll automatically dial that number or go to that website? If you have something like that—a powerful web address that will automatically steer customers to your site—then you might have something of value to offer; but chances are, at this late stage, it would be awfully difficult to find one.

More commonly, the valuable asset that makes an Internet business licensable is a proprietary software program that makes the business work and isn't available to the competition. Amazon is famous for developing a "one-click" software program that makes buying easy and led them to quickly outpace all of their competitors, who are still trying to catch up. So yes, certainly you need to do some research to show that your Internet business idea has potential, but that's the easy part. If your web business idea is to sell fishing supplies, it's easy to show that there are 30 million fisherman (or whatever), but nobody is going to license another fishing products website unless you have something unique and proprietary to offer that gives your licensee a selling edge—something that sets your licensee's business apart from all the competitors selling the same products.

Now that you've determined that your idea is truly original and has enough commercial value to continue with its development, this is a good time to start thinking about the type of legal protection it might need before you get it (and yourself) prepared to meet the folks with the checkbooks who are waiting for your call. All will be revealed in the next chapter.

3

THE END OF THE FREE RIDE

All About Patents and the Lawyers Who Are Happy to Sell You One

You were born to be a winner, but to be a winner you must plan to win, prepare to win, expect to win.

—Zig Ziglar, sales expert

This is the section where we have to talk about lawyers and patents and things like that, so hold on to you wallets and I'll try to make it as painless as possible. First, let's take a look at the kinds of legal protections that are available.

UTILITY PATENT

This is applicable for the invention or creation of a basic new process, machine, manufacture, or composition of matter. The idea must be primary, useful, original, and operational. Utility patents are designed to provide 17 years of exclusive use for the idea that's covered. What a utility patent actually is, however, is simply a passkey to the courthouse. If someone copies your patent, you can't call the Patent Police and have the rat thrown in jail. You have to get a lawyer and sue him in court. But remember, rats have lawyers too (more on that unpleasant thought later).

Confidentially, just as an aside, I know of some small companies that make little novelty products and automatically put "patent pending" on all of their product packages, even though they've never seen a patent application in their lives. They figure, "What the heck? There are no patent-pending police, and so if the warning scares off a few competitors, why not?" The problem is, since their competitors do the same unsavory thing themselves, the notice scares off no one who is determined to make a copycat item. If you see a package for a lapel flower that shoots water or a phony dead fly in a fake ice cube, and if the package says, "patent pending," it doesn't take a brilliant mind to know that no sane person would spend the money to file a patent for something like that. Fortunately, these companies are the exception, not the norm. Overwhelmingly, the "patent pending" warning on a package means what it says and does the job that it's intended for. "Patent pending" on the package does not give the manufacturer the legal right to stop others from copycatting, but it does warn that if and when an actual patent is issued, that right comes along with it.

PLANT PATENT

Quoting a government booklet, "The law provides for the granting of a patent to anyone who has invented or discovered an asexually reproduced and distinct and new variety of plant, including cultured spores, mutants, hybrids, and newly found seedlings, other than tuber-propagated plants or a plant found in an uncultured state." I couldn't say it better myself. The Patent and Trademark office, which is part of the Department of Commerce, will usually require that an exhibit accompany this type of application, unlike other patent applications. As with the utility patent, the protection is for 17 years.

DESIGN PATENT

This patent offers protection for a unique, ornamental design of the exterior of the product. It has nothing to do with how the product works, only with how it looks.

For instance, Auguste Bartholdi, the sculptor, had a design patent on the Statue of Liberty. It's not uncommon for a company to have both a utility patent on how their product works and a design patent for how it looks. However, unless the precise design of the product is critical to the product's success, this kind of patent has limited value.

PROVISIONAL PATENT APPLICATION

This is the newest patent protection device offered by the Patent Office, and it's specifically designed to help the private, individual inventor. As you can tell by the name, this is not a patent, per se; it's designed for temporary protection to give the inventor time (one year) to decide if his or her invention warrants the investment in one of the traditional patents. What the provisional patent does is save your place in line. In other words, let's suppose you invented a new kind of bread box and got a provisional patent for it. And let's suppose an agent from the evil bread box cartel sees your design and rushes to the Patent Office to start the process for getting a utility patent himself for the very same product. And then let's assume that five months later, you, too, decide to get a utility patent on your bread box. The fact that the year hasn't expired and you're still under the protection of your provisional patent, allows you to say to the nefarious bread box thief, "Hey! I was here first!" And the Patent Office will agree, throwing the bum out into the street.

The good news is that this is really cheap protection ($100 the last time I checked) and it's something you can do without a lawyer. Further good news is that it permits you to put "patent pending" warning notices on all your material, and whoever sees it doesn't know if you have a provisional patent or if what's pending is a conventional patent application. The bad news is that, when the year is up, that's it—there are no extensions. There have been many complaints about the brevity of the protection and the Patent Office is looking for ways to extend it. However, that hasn't happened yet, so after the year, if you haven't filed for a regular patent, your protection vanishes. But what the heck, whether they extend the time or not, it's so cheap to buy this protection, why not do it?

BUSINESS MODEL PATENT

The United States is one of the few countries that considers certain types of business methods to be intellectual property and therefore protectable by patent. In order to obtain patent protection on your method of doing business, it must meet three standards. First, you have to prove that your method of doing business is "novel." You would have previously done an exhaustive search of existing business model patents and applications (which are also published) to justify the claim that no other patented business model or application duplicates or critically resembles your own. Second, you have to claim and demonstrate that this business method is a practical and useful application that's essential to the business and is not just an abstract idea or concept. Finally, you must claim and demonstrate that your method is imaginative and would not be obvious to others in the same industry. This is new and evolving law, often including software that makes the business model function— and it would be difficult for a private inventor to make a successful application without the help of an experienced intellectual property attorney.

TRADEMARKS

Using the Patent Office definition, "A trademark may be a word, symbol, design, or combination words and design, a slogan or even a distinctive sound, which identifies the goods and services of one party from another."

Coke and Pepsi are trademarks, of course, but so is the roar from a Harley-Davidson motorcycle. The motor on a Harley has a distinctive sound, and anyone who knows motorcycles can hear and identify a Harley even before the bike comes into view. Harley was able to get a trademark for that distinctive sound because, they argued, it was distinctive to their brand. Lots of things carry a trademark that we'd never think of, such as the pink used in Fiberglass insulation or the roar of the MGM lion.

Selecting and owning the right trademarked name for a product is so important that at least a dozen professional name development research companies exist to provide that service to industry. One of the main ones is NameQuest, Inc. (www.namequest.com), and here's a quote from the president, John Hoeppner: "The goal of effective verbal brand naming is to choose a product name that reflects and fits the customer's needs so precisely that the name sells the product."

A trademark can be a hugely valuable asset, so if you have a name for your product, service, or game show that uniquely describes it in a memorable way, the few hundred dollars it costs to protect it might produce great rewards down the road. That little "TM" you see beside a name signifies that it's trademark protected.

COPYRIGHTS

Patents and trademarks are issued by the Patent Office, but copyrights are under the jurisdiction of the Library of Congress because they're designed to protect artistic and literary works. "Literary and artistic works" doesn't just mean paintings and books; it also covers such diverse works as movies, plays, songs, cartoon characters, and so on.

It can also protect any software you might develop, or the copy and look of a website you might design, or your description of that brilliant game show idea you have in mind. Unlike a patent, which has a relatively short expiration date, a copyright is in force for the life of the creator, plus 70 years. That's why Elvis is still a top money earner.

Any creative effort of yours, regardless of the form, automatically has copyright protection without you doing anything. If someone copies your drawing or your song or anything else, you have the right to take that person to court to make him stop. However, if you officially register your material with the Library of Congress and pay the required fee, not only can you use the courts to make the copier stop, you might also be able to collect for any monetary damages you suffered because of the theft.

PROTECTING YOUR NEW PRODUCT IDEA

Years ago I dreamed up a clever little product called Sip'n Lips. Did you ever buy a pair of those funny wax lips when you were a kid? These lips are usually sold around Halloween time and come in big red lipstick lips for girls and gory fang lips for boys. And do you know those straws that are all twisty and curly those sort of take a drink on a rollercoaster ride from the glass before it enters the mouth? All I did was make these lips out of plastic instead of wax and attached one of those curly straws to it. The idea was to make it fun for a child to drink his or her milk. It was an easy product to dream up, easy to license, and easy for the licensee to get placement in retail stores. It was just a cute little carded impulse item that sold for a few dollars. Not a big deal by any standards.

At no point did the thought of obtaining a patent for this product enter my mind, or the licensee's mind, or the minds of the retailers. I knew I didn't need a patent to license this idea because I knew the licensee wouldn't demand it. It wasn't worth the money to get the patent, and it certainly wouldn't be worth the money to defend it if a copycat emerged on the scene (none ever did). There are lots of perfectly decent and profitable products in the marketplace that have no patent because the investment isn't worth it. If your product is cheap and easy to make, and if it will probably have a short life span, such as a toy, novelty item, or a little giftware product, then save your money. A patent won't be asked for by the licensee, and having one will do little to sway his licensing decision. What is of value is being first—and if it's a good product, that privilege is worth a licensing deal to the company.

The kind of products I tend to create are largely of the Sip'n Lips variety, and over the years, I've licensed more than a hundred products of this sort to various companies. None of my created products was ever patented—and while not everyone bought what I offered,

I was never turned down for the lack of having a patent on the product idea I was presenting.

On the other hand, if your product idea will require a substantial tooling investment, and if it's intended to remain in the marketplace for a long time, then having a patent would probably be required. A company would think twice about entering into a licensing agreement, making a substantial tooling investment and creating the market for a product, knowing that their competitors can do the same thing for free. In fact, large companies won't even look at an inventor's idea unless it's patented.

One of those invention companies might charge you thousands of dollars to secure a patent on your product, and if your idea doesn't qualify for a utility patent, either because some similar patented entity already exists or the idea itself is too commonplace, they may instead get a design patent for your product. They can always get a design for their inventor clients, even while knowing in their cold hearts that it's probably worthless. As already indicated, except in rare cases where the design itself is essential to the product's success, these patents have little value. There are exceptions, of course. One example that comes to mind are those little pine-tree-shaped air fresheners that hang from a car's rearview mirror. This design, being essential to the product's commercial success, does have a design patent (and is worth every penny). It's that singular tree design that everyone thinks of when they think of car air fresheners. In most instances, however, one nice product design is pretty much as good as the next one.

When an inventor refers to a patent, it's almost always a utility patent that he or she has in mind—but having a utility patent awarded can take years (20 months is the average) and applying can be very expensive. You can get a design patent on your own, or a trademark or a copyright on your own, but to get a utility patent that's strong enough to matter, I believe you really need an expert to write it. I know there are books and software programs designed to help you apply for a utility patent on your own, and following their instructions you might do a great job. But chances are you won't be as thorough as a professional, and you might come to regret it. If your product is on the market, selling well, and if a competitor company wants to make its own version, the first thing that company will do is study your patent to look for ways around it. If you're going to invest in a patent at all, it should be the best that you can get.

It's precisely because applying for a utility patent is so expensive and time consuming (and so often unnecessary) that the U.S. Patent and Trademark office came up with the concept of the provisional patent application. They know better than anyone what a long, expensive process it is to get a utility patent, and they know that often it turns out to be a needless expense. During the one-year grace period that a provisional patent provides, the inventor wanting to market his invention himself might find the market too tough, or the inventor looking for a licensee might find no interest, and so the time and the thousands of dollars that might otherwise been spent for full legal protection can be saved.

First of all, since applying for a provisional patent is so cheap, and since it's something you can do yourself, I recommend everyone who has a product idea do it—if for no other reason than it buys you the right to put a "patent pending" notice on your product material while you're shopping it around. It couldn't hurt. As already noted, putting a "patent pending" notice on a product offers no immediate protection other than to warn that if and when the patent is issued, any company that has invested in tooling to copy the product might regret it. That's pretty good protection when it costs only about a hundred dollars.

Also, I should point out that, frankly speaking, having a provisional patent does little to impress a potential licensee. The licensee prospect knows that a provisional patent application is not examined by the patent office, and so no value judgment has been made as to whether it could actually earn a real patent. Anyone with the money to pay the fee can get a provisional patent. You can get a provisional patent for a ham sandwich. For the type of product idea that doesn't require a patent anyway, it doesn't matter. If your invention is for the kind of product that should have a utility patent, I suggest the combination of a provisional patent and an attorney's opinion letter that the idea is patentable. That way, if the licensee wants to go ahead with a licensing deal, he has your contractual agreement to file for a utility patent and the attorney's opinion that it will be awarded.

America is what's known as a "first to invent" country—meaning if you apply for a utility patent for a particular product, and someone else also applies for the same product, if you can prove that you were the first to invent it, your application would take precedence. Some people send a registered letter to themselves in which they describe their idea. When the letter arrives it's kept unopened, with the postmark date on the envelope being proof of the date of invention. It's what they call a "poor man's patent." That might work as part of a preponderance of evidence being presented to the court but probably not on its own since a clever person might be able to tamper with the envelope in an almost undetectable fashion. Better evidence is an inventor's log in which you would enter little sketches and comments about the product's development from day to day. A diagonal line should be drawn from the last word on the page down to the bottom to prevent further entries, and each page should be witnessed, dated, and signed by someone who has no interest in the success of the product. Any school notebook will do the job, as long as it's bound so that pages can't later be added or removed.

PROTECTING YOUR SOFTWARE IDEA

There's no protection for the software idea as such. No matter how brilliant the idea is, the protection is in the doing. The source code for your software program meets the court's requirements to be protected by law as a trade secret if:

1. The secret is valuable to the business. Presumably your source code would be considered to be valuable since it's for software that performs a function.

2. You can demonstrate that you've kept the code as a secret—not making it public and not showing it to anyone except on a need-to-know basis.

3. You can demonstrate to the courts that no one other than yourself or others involved in the development of the software have knowledge of the code and that they have signed nondisclosure agreements. In other words, if you want the court to view your code as a secret, you have to show that you are rigidly protecting it as such.

A trade secret is intellectual property, and as such, it can be sold or licensed. Unlike conventional patents, which have a limited life, a trade secret as intellectual property can last indefinitely as long as it's kept as such. The classic example is Coca-Cola, which has maintained its formula as a trade secret since the company was started in 1892. If I contrived to steal the Coca-Cola secret formula and was caught, that would be a theft or attempted theft, and I would be viewed in the courts as a criminal.

Ideas are ephemeral; anyone can have them. It would be chaos if people could copyright ideas—we would then have thought police roaming the countryside. However, while the idea for the software program itself cannot be legally protected, what you do with the idea certainly can be. It would be difficult to come up with a software idea that would be wholly original, but how you put that idea into practice, in some new and novel way—such as producing software that perhaps achieves better information or results in an easier and quicker fashion—can be wholly original and capable of being protected.

Software law is constantly evolving and a whole body of lawyers now exists who have been specially trained as intellectual property law practitioners. Many of these attorneys are based in San Francisco and the Silicon Valley for obvious reasons. I had a lengthy meeting with one of the better-known ones in San Francisco, David Tollen of Adeli & Tollen (www.AdeliTollen.com), who explained that every software application, as soon as it's put on disk, automatically enjoys copyright protection. However, just as with other copyrighted material, if the developer officially files for protection, he or she might enjoy broader rights in the courts. The automatic copyright gives you the right to petition the court to make an infringer desist, but if it's an officially filed copyright, you might also get the court to order the infringer to pay your attorney fees (which can be astronomical in a software infringement case), court costs, and what are called "statutory damages" up to $100,000 per infringement without even the need to prove your damages.

If you want to file on your own, it's fast, cheap, and easy. The last time I checked, the fee was less than $50 and the form is simple—asking the title of the work, who developed it, and who owns it—and you have to include two copies of the copyrighted work with the application. A sample form is in the Appendix. However, if only for your own piece of mind, I believe you should have a professional do the filing to ensure all of your rights and the program's secrets are properly protected.

It has long been known that software programs can be protected by copyright, but as mentioned, a copyright protects only the expression of an idea, not the idea itself. Consequently, more and more owners of major software programs use patents (if they qualify) for added protection. In order to obtain a patent, the software has to meet the requirements of being new, useful, and not obvious; but since none of those requirements are hard and fast, with the court offering ill-defined boundaries between patentable and non-patentable, I believe a legal expert would be needed to determine the software's qualifications and to make the case in the filing to the examiners.

However, while a utility patent can provide broader protection than a copyright—perhaps protecting the program's algorithm or preventing others from developing a software program that does a function in a particular way—making a patent application is an expensive process with uncertain results. Moreover, not every software program is of magnitude to warrant that kind of investment. Just as lots of types of regular products don't warrant the investment in a utility patent, it is also true for many software programs, where the much-cheaper-to-get copyright is all the protection that's appropriate.

For instance, I have an iPhone app that sells for a few dollars: "My Invention." The app user answers a series of multiple choice questions about the nature and status of his or her product idea, and depending on the responses, the program offers a collection of suggested next steps to take. The software is generic and there's nothing exceptional about the layout or how it works. Furthermore, although the information this program offers is valuable for the right person, in terms of commercial potential, the market is small. The copyright protection on this product is all that's needed.

Even if this app had potential for patenting (unlikely), it's clearly not worth the investment. However, if I wasn't marketing this app myself, I could have probably licensed it to a competitor because, as with many software programs, its value is in the doing. "My Invention" is a finished, tested product producing worthwhile results. The investment in time, money, and creativity has already been made. The licensee could simply put his name on it and instantly be the wise product guru—all it would cost him is a small royalty to be paid on each one sold.

PROTECTING YOUR TV GAME OR REALITY SHOW IDEA

Patents and copyrights do not protect ideas, and since what you have in this instance is simply an idea, the available protection is meager. Moreover, it is highly unlikely that anyone to whom you might tell this idea—a production company or TV executive—will sign a nondisclosure agreement. That's not because they intend to steal your idea (hopefully), but because they're in the business of hearing ideas, hundreds of them, all day long, and they couldn't logically confine themselves to what they hear. Your idea might be original, but it's not likely to be so original that there aren't echoes of it in current reality shows or those from the past, or in the minds of others pitching their own reality show ideas. What you hope to have is a novel take or a new twist, and that might be all you need. No one expects your idea to be really new; what they're hoping is that it's new enough, with its own clever take to set it apart. The same would supply to a game show. There have been more game shows on TV than one can count, but that doesn't mean there isn't always room for something fresh, original, and entertaining.

Although there are some protection steps that should be taken, which I'll explain, the real protection is the fact that the production company or TV network executive is not listening to your idea with the expectation of stealing it. If what you are suggesting is truly original, interesting, and commercially valuable, it's a lot simpler and more sensible to work out a deal with you as the creator than to potentially subject themselves to a nasty lawsuit. Not only might it be expensive, but who's going to bring them new ideas if they have a reputation for stealing them?

You will, of course, have a copyright on the narrative of your show but, as already mentioned, not on the idea itself. Those are ephemeral. What most TV writers and show developers do is register their work with the TV Writers Vault (CreatorsVault.com) or with the Writers Guild of America West (WGAWRegistry.org), both of whom offer a time-stamped proof of creation. Registration is cheap, less than $40, and you can do it right from your computer. Any registered material presented to a TV network or production company executive would have that notice of registration printed on it, so presumably they'd think twice if they had any funny ideas. You should also have (and register) what's called a log line for your show (covered later) and a few pages describing how the show would work, the host, the number of contestants, its locale, its dramatic arc, and how it's concluded, meaning the rewards or outcome. You might also offer a suggested structure of a typical episode. You'd not be expected to actually write a script, just a clear description of the show itself. You also need a title for your show. The title can't be legally protected (just as it isn't for books and movies) but it's a handy way to refer to the work. I won't kid you—this type of protection is not iron clad—but it is what it is: a way to keep honest people honest.

Further, if your show requires certain unique equipment that you've invented, or a software program that you created to make the show work in a certain unique way, you can, of course, protect those elements either by patent or copyright. For the most part, however, if you want to pitch your reality show idea or game show idea to the television industry, you have to rely on the kindness (and honesty) of strangers and get comfort in knowing-that stealing your show is not in their best interests.

PROTECTING YOUR INTERNET BUSINESS IDEA

The idea of simply taking a business that has customarily been conducted from a store front and moving it online is not in itself anything likely to attract an interested licensee. He can do that himself; he doesn't need us. In order for the idea to have licensing value, the business idea has to contain one or more unique secret or proprietary assets that would give the licensee a strong, exclusive advantage over the inevitable copycat businesses. What this unique advantage might be takes several forms. You might have created a unique software program to make the business work more efficiently than your competitors can, or you might have a captive source for the material to be sold, or a patented machine to product the product, or a trade secret that might be a formula or recipe, or perhaps a powerful web address. Each of these assets can be protected in its own way, and any of these might be enough to make your business proposal interesting to a potential licensee. But you need something—or else this might be a good time to start refocusing your creativity in other directions.

The most common asset that can make an Internet business idea licensable is the development of a unique software program that might, for instance, allow order fulfillment to be done faster, cheaper, and easier than a competitor might do it. As already mentioned, the patented software for Amazon's "one-click" customer ordering system is a prime example. Recently, patent laws have been expanded to include unique business methods, even if they didn't involve a computer, just so they produced a "useful, concrete, and tangible" result. However, the reality is that a business method patent currently takes several years before being issued, if ever, and only then can the owner stop a competitor from employing the same method. Quite possibly by then—who cares?

If the way you've designed the web pages on this proposed business is so clever or original that customers would prefer shopping at this site over the competitors' sites, then your copyright on the website layout might be enough to pique a licensee's interest. Or, if what you're proposing to sell is desirable and in limited supply, and if you can show that you have unique access to this supply, that too could certainly interest a potential licensee.

For instance, the artist Thomas Kinkaid is very popular and lots of folks happily buy his paintings and prints. If you had a special relationship with Mr. Kinkaid, giving you first rights to sell his artistic output, it would certainly be a valuable asset. Also, again using that example, if you owned the website "ThomasKinkaidArt.com" that, too, would be uniquely valuable—or Horseshoes.com if you were selling horseshoes. Either one might qualify as a valid trademark.

Some years ago I was involved with the then famous and enormously successful Hooked on Phonics children's reading program—which at the time was so heavily advertised on radio and TV that it was hard to miss. Before launching his company, John Shanahan, the fellow who dreamed it up, called 1-800-222-3334, which as I recall was a fencing company, and offered them $10,000 for the number. That was a princely sum at the time. He didn't buy 1-800-222-3334—what he bought was 1-800-A-B-C-D-E-F-G, which he attached to a little jingle and made it the basis for the millions he spent on advertising. There was hardly anyone in the United States over the age of 10 who didn't know that number by heart. And when he sold the company, the website ABCDEFG.com was and still is a valuable asset.

You might also have applied for and received a patent on the business method of running your proposed business. This would require long-range planning since it usually takes about two years before such a patent would be awarded, if it at all. In the meantime, your application is published, open for anyone to see—and until a patent is actually granted, there's no way to stop copycats. For instance, Netflix received a patent for their unique film rental method and within hours of having the patent officially awarded they initiated suit against Blockbuster for patent infringement.

YES, BUT IS YOUR PRODUCT OR SOFTWARE PROTECTED IN BULGARIA?

A treaty called the Paris Convention joins most of the world's industrialized nations. Essentially this gives an individual inventor, after filing for a patent in one of the member countries (usually his own), the right to file in any or all other member countries within a year, using the date of his original filing. For instance, let's say that you filed for a patent in the United States, licensed your product, and the licensee had the product on the market within four months. And now let's say that a French manufacturer saw the product, liked it, and decided to copy it and apply for a French patent. If a few months later, you too decide to apply for a French patent, and if it's within a year of filing for your U.S. patent, your filing will take precedence over the French company's application.

As a practical matter, filing for world patents is out of reach for most private inventors. The costs are so high, the process so complicated, and the defense so expensive that it's seldom a sensible, affordable, or necessary move. The American domestic market is so huge and is so small in most other countries, that it usually doesn't pay for a local foreign manufacturer to produce a copycat product and file for a patent in his own country if he's blocked from selling elsewhere.

Further, if you've licensed your product to a large U.S. company with worldwide distribution, and if your invention has enough significance, you can probably get the company itself to do the filing. Large companies have patent attorneys on their staff or at least on retainer, so filing for foreign patents is routine and holds no mystery for them. The filing would be done in your name as the inventor, and you'd assign your licensee the rights. Another scenario might be that your licensee only sells in the United States. You might then approach the French manufacturer yourself and make a licensing deal with them for their own marketing area.

Similarly, there's the Universal Copyright Convention and the Berne Convention, whereby the member nations agree to honor the copyrights awarded by any other member country.

BEWARE OF THE PERILS OF JOINT OWNERSHIP

If you and your brother-in-law, Fat Melvin, file for a patent as co-inventors, as far as the Patent Office is concerned, you are equal partners. The Patent Office doesn't care that you did 90 percent of the work while Fat Melvin just sat there eating Hostess Twinkies. The only partnership percentage that the Patent Office knows is 50–50. Each of you owns the patent, and either of you can act independently, awarding usage rights to the patent to one entity or another without the joint owner's permission. It doesn't take much imagination to envision the problems that can arise, so if joint ownership can't be avoided, you and your co-owner should at least have a separate agreement between you about the patent's usage and the division of proceeds.

If the development of your product idea requires technical skills that you might not have, and if acquiring the services of someone who does have those skills is expensive, you might think of offering him or her a partnership in the patent in exchange for the technical contribution. My advice is—don't. File for the patent on your own as the sole inventor and give the other person an agreement that promises half the profits—but don't make him or her a co-inventor. That's just asking for trouble.

It's a natural tendency for people to look for partners whenever they embark on a new venture. There's comfort in having a person to share the chores with and to discuss matters with—and it gives many people the courage to press forward that they might not have on their own. However, the reality is that most private partnerships eventually fail, often leaving bitterness on both sides. I've been in partnerships twice in my career, and both times the relationship didn't end well. The problem wasn't that my partners were bad or dishonest—they weren't—but the pressures of making every decision jointly usually just becomes too much. No two of us think the same way about everything and friction is inevitable. So if you don't absolutely, positively need to make your brother-in-law Fat Melvin a partner on your invention, don't do it.

SOMETHING ELSE TO KNOW

In an average year more than 200,000 patent applications are received by the U.S. Patent and Trademark Office and a little better than half of them are granted. And, as earlier mentioned, the average waiting time is 20 months. These are not wonderful statistics, considering the fact that even the simplest utility patent application will probably cost $10,000 with no upper limit. Nevertheless, if what you've invented is valuable, it might deserve the strongest protection that you can get. Settling for less could one day break your heart.

THE PAPER TRAIL

Sometimes you need a lawyer to help protect your idea and sometimes you don't, but either way, what you always need to do is leave a paper trail. The courts usually find that if you present a new and novel idea to a company—something that wouldn't be obvious to them in the normal course of running their business—and if they can't prove that it's an idea long known to them or that logically would be known by them, then they have an obligation not to attempt to use the idea themselves. This is not hard-and-fast law, but if you have the proof of your dealings with this company, and if they obviously acted in an unscrupulous way, judges will usually find in your favor. This proof of dealings is what's called a *paper trail*.

Let's suppose you read somewhere that most women prefer turquoise over any other color, and let's suppose you went to the Ajax Steam Iron Company and made the suggestion that they make the handles on their steam irons in a turquoise color—asking them for a royalty on each steam iron they sell with the colored handle. "Thanks, kid," they said, as they had security escort you from the building. And now let's suppose that six months later, while visiting a store, you see a big display of the new Ajax steam irons, all with turquoise handles. Those crummy rats! They stole your idea! "Not so fast," the judge will probably say. "This is the kind of information that would have easily come to the attention of Ajax without you telling them, and so they don't owe you a dime." Ajax might still be crummy rats, but not for making steam irons with turquoise handles.

On the other hand, if you invented some amazing new type of iron handle that can switch around for lefties and switch the other way for righties and that automatically plays music while the person is ironing, and if Ajax just swiped the idea, the same judge who told you to get lost when you complained about the turquoise handles might make those crummy rats pay for the theft. But you'll need the paper trail of evidence to show that you're the one who gave Ajax the idea and the design.

If you met with Mr. Smedley from Ajax to show him your Switcheroo musical iron handle, you'd follow with a letter:

Dear Mr. Smedley,

It was nice meeting with you on Tuesday, May 10, and I'm pleased with your favorable reaction to my new Switcheroo musical handle idea for your steam irons—and I'm delighted that you requested I leave my prototype so you could show this exciting idea to your colleagues. As you suggested, I'll call you next Thursday to discuss our next steps together.

Or if Smedley said he didn't like the idea, you'd still send him a follow-up letter, expressing your disappointment that he didn't like your amazing new Switcheroo musical handle. No matter what transpired at the meeting, good or bad, the essence of the letter is confirmation that you introduced Smedley to your new Switcheroo musical handle on such-and-such a date. Smedley will know you're not sending this letter because your mother taught you such good manners; he knows exactly why you're sending the letter. That's fine. That's the whole point: You're telling him that you're no one to mess with.

No matter what subsequent contacts you have with Smedley or anyone else at Ajax about the Switcheroo musical handle, a phone call, an e-mail, a fax, another meeting—whatever—it should always be followed up by a written confirmation, a copy of which is placed in your files. Gypsy Rose Lee, the famous burlesque queen, once said, "God is love, but have it in writing." Let that be your guide. I do this automatically, even with companies that I've been dealing with for years—and never has one of these companies tried to pull a fast one.

Oh, and one more thing: It wouldn't hurt for you to create a nice letterhead for yourself on your computer and use that in your correspondence with Smedley. It seems to make everything more official. Also, have a little chat with your accountant. It might not be a bad idea to set up a separate checking account to pay for all the bills associated with your inventing and licensing—lawyers' fees, prototype costs, travel, and so on. All of these expenses might be tax deductible.

WHEN YOU REALLY DO NEED A LAWYER, HERE'S HOW TO FIND THE RIGHT ONE

First, all things being equal, you probably should avoid the big, fancy firms. Or, more accurately, they will probably avoid you. Most of these large intellectual property firms are interested in corporate accounts where the business is on a continuing basis, not one-shot individual inventors who will wince at their fees. To them, you're one notch above pro bono. And even if, in the goodness of their hearts they do decide to take you on, you'll probably be assigned to the youngest, newest attorney on staff who will use you as practice. Unless you like being the practice dummy, I suggest moving on.

If your product is simple, requiring a simple patent, then probably any good patent lawyer with a medium to small practice can do the job. However, if your product is highly complicated or technical, or if your software idea is particularly complex, you probably need a lawyer whose schooling will enable him to easily grasp the significance of your accomplishment. Patent lawyers need an engineering degree before a legal degree, and as you know, there are all sorts of engineers: electrical, mechanical, chemical, electronic, and so on. You should probably work with a lawyer whose training complements the nature of your invention.

Since selecting the right attorney for you is such a subjective matter, it pays to get whatever guidance and recommendations are available. Joining a local inventors club can be a valuable source for this type of help. Membership fees are nominal, and membership gives you the opportunity to chat with fellow inventors who will be happy to share their own experiences with various patent attorneys that they've used themselves. Further, these clubs usually meet monthly and the guest speaker is frequently a local patent attorney, giving you a casual way to meet and chat before deciding if you want to proceed with the formalities of an office meeting. I've spoken at several of these clubs over the years and found the atmosphere very collegial. Inventing is usually a solitary business, so it's nice to meet others who are similarly engaged. A list of these clubs is in the Appendix.

Further, you should keep in mind that because of the aggressive advertising that many lawyers do, making it as much of a business as a profession, you should consider yourself a customer, shopping around, looking for a good deal. You'd probably check out two or three roofers to get a new roof, so why not do the same with lawyers? Most first meetings with a lawyer are free, and this is where you can ask their billing methods, their hourly rate, and what they estimate the cost will be for the invention that you put on their desk. Many will offer a flat fee, whereas others might offer an estimate. Either way, you'll leave the office with some idea of the costs involved in dealing with one attorney or another, and you'll have a sense of whether he or she is a lawyer that you would be at ease working with. And don't worry about fully disclosing your idea. All patent attorneys are legally bound to hold your invention in strict confidence, whether you use their services or not.

If an attorney, instead of offering a flat fee, intends to bill you for his services, in addition to asking his hourly rate, it would be interesting to know his billable unit. Most attorneys use six minutes as a billable unit because it conveniently divides the hour by 10. Others, however, will use 15 minutes. That's an important difference. A billable unit is the minimum time the attorney will charge for whatever is asked of him by a client. Let's say both attorneys have a $300 hourly rate. If you make a quick four-minute call to the attorney with the six-minute billable unit, the cost will be $30 (10 percent of the hourly rate). If you make the same call to the other attorney who uses a 15-minute unit, the cost will be $75 (25 percent of his hourly rate). That's a big difference when you consider how many calls there might be between you and your attorney while he's preparing your patent application.

One other caveat: Now that you're the client, when you meet with your attorney, have a prepared list of questions you need to have answered so when you know what you came to his office to learn, you can shake his hand and leave. Talk is cheap, but not when you're talking to an attorney. If you want to tell him the latest jokes or the cute things your young child did, he'll laugh appreciatively, but the clock is ticking.

Rule #6: Don't tell jokes to an attorney who's billing you by the hour.

Also, instead of a patent attorney you might want to give consideration to engaging a patent agent. Patent agents might be just as qualified to write a great patent filing as the attorney and they work much cheaper. Patent agents are officially recognized by the Patent Office and so are legally eligible to write and file the patent application for you. The principal difference is that since they're not attorneys, they can't offer legal advice or defend you in a lawsuit. If that doesn't matter, if you're just looking for qualified help in filing the patent, then they're worth your consideration.

The Step-by-Step Patent Application Process and How You're Billed Every Step of the Way

If you're comparing prices from several attorneys, then knowing the process will be useful. There are a minimum of five billable portions to the patent application process and more if there's a back-and-forth dispute between your attorney and the patent examiner.

1.   The search

2.   Government filing fees

3.   Drawings (depending on how many are needed)

4.   Out-of-pocket expenses

5.   Professional services

The first four charges won't vary much from attorney to attorney. First, most lawyers don't do the search themselves; they'll hire an outside search firm and mark up the costs. Second, the filing fees are what they are. Third, there are freelance art specialists who know how to draw an invention to accurately explain it in a way to meet the Patent Office formalities. Your attorney will discuss the invention with one of these specialists and they'll decide between them how many drawings are necessary. The specialist will charge the lawyer, who will mark up the costs and charge you. Fourth, out-of-pocket expenses are incidental costs, such as for duplicating, mailings, and so on. Fifth, professional services is where the lawyer earns his keep and where the fees from one lawyer to another might be so far apart that you'll think they're not both from the same planet. Which one to use is largely a judgment call, and it pretty much comes down to whom you trust and whom you're more comfortable working with.

The professional services are about the skill, time, and talent that the attorney uses to draft the claims for your invention and his ability to convince the examiner that each claim is a valid one. Each claim is for a portion of your invention that is offered as being new and original and that therefore should belong to you alone. The stronger the claims that surround your invention, like the strength of the walls around a castle, the less likely they'll be breached. If the attorney does a good job, your patent will be defensible; and if he doesn't, it won't. So make sure you're working with someone you trust, even if he doesn't laugh at your jokes.

Oh, and One More Thing About Lawyers

If you're dealing with an attorney whom you like and trust (overwhelmingly, patent attorneys are honorable individuals) and if the patent application is going to be a large, expensive amount of work, a patent attorney might be interested in providing professional services (including negotiating a deal) for a percentage of potential profits. I'm told that this type of arrangement is against a Bar Association code of ethics because the attorney, by virtue of his training, might have an unfair advantage over the inventor, but I know for a fact that these types of arrangements do exist. There are so many variables that I can't advise if this type of arrangement is right for you or not, or even if your attorney would be interested in a deal like this, but if you think this type of arrangement might be attractive, it can't hurt to bring up the subject.

But enough about patents and lawyers and things that go bump in the night. Let's move on to the fun part—getting your brilliant idea prepped and ready to show to the person who's going to put your name up in lights.

4

It's Time to Swing into Action (The Devil Is in the Details)

How to Prepare Your Presentation Material in a Way That Will Knock Their Socks Off

The critical ingredient is getting off your butt and doing something. It's as simple as that. A lot of people have ideas but few of them do anything with them now, not tomorrow, not next week, but today. Be a doer, not a dreamer.

—Nolan Bushnell, Inventor of Pong, founder of Atari

About 70 years ago, so the legend goes, a teenage beauty named Lana Turner was sipping a soda at Schwab's drugstore on the corner of Hollywood and Vine (drugstores had soda fountains in those days) when a big-time producer came up and offered to put her in pictures and make her a star—and he did. That probably was the last time in history that anyone succeeded by just sitting there doing nothing. Today you have to push and shove and hustle and yell, "Look at me!" if you want to get anywhere.

A mediocre idea that has been licensed is a million times better than a brilliant idea that's gathering dust on a shelf, waiting to be discovered. Forget Lana Turner—nothing happens nowadays until you go out and sell something. And like any good salesperson, you're not going to hit the road until you're sure you have the tools you need to get the order. What I mean, of course, is the presentation material for your idea. No matter how sophisticated the executive might be to whom you're showing your invention, he'll pay more attention to good looking, professionally prepared presentation material than he will to something amateurish. The quality of your presentation material reflects on the idea and on you as its developer. Doing it right is money well spent.

Since we know companies don't buy dreams, the essential aim of a good presentation is to position the product or business idea or game show idea as something that is far removed from simply a dream, but rather as something approaching reality. You don't want to say, "Here's what I think my idea *could* do"; you want your presentation to say, "Here's what my product *will* do," or "Here's how my game show will play," or "Here's how my Internet business *will* operate." It's never "could," it's always "will." The subtle suggestion being made to the prospective customer or licensee is that "This train is leaving the station. If you want to be left on the platform, that's up to you."

PREPARING YOUR PRODUCT INVENTION

Regardless of what your product idea is, you have to bring it up to a certain level of completion for two reasons. First, if your idea warrants some type of legal protection, such as a patent or a copyright, you have to know in some detail what it is that you want to have protected. It would be pointless to apply for a patent for a product that has not yet been thoroughly designed and proven to work. And second, you have to put your idea into the prospective licensee's hands at a level of completion that he has a right to expect before committing to a licensing deal. Also, since in your absence the executive will often want to discuss this new idea with colleagues before agreeing to a deal, you want him to be well equipped to get a collective favorable reaction. If the company executive says to you, "Hey! I like that idea! Let's see how it works," are you just going to give him a blank stare? I don't think so.

As I know I've already said and re-said—nobody licenses ideas. Send a company an idea and you'll get a boilerplate "thank you for your suggestion" note in return. If the Wright Brothers tried to get money from a company just by saying they thought they could invent something heavier than air that could fly, they'd probably be told, "Yeah, sure, come back when you guys are sober." Of course, with an actual plane to show them, and after Kitty Hawk to provide the validity of their idea, it was a different story.

It's not the idea—we all get ideas—it's what the inventor does with the idea that might pique the interest of a potential licensee. The level of completion that's required to gain interest varies with the type of project and the requirements of the industry (and a lot of common sense). If your nephew Jeffrey comes to you with a "brilliant" product idea for you to invest in, but you've always been a little leery that Jeffrey might not be the sharpest knife in the drawer, the first thing you'll do is ask to see what he's talking about. If Jeffrey says, "Trust me, Unc; this thing is terrific!" your checkbook will remain in the drawer. You want to see for yourself what this thing looks like, how it works, how it is made, how it is better than the competition, and so forth. Companies are no different. To them you're Jeffrey.

It's always better to have a working prototype than not to have one. Someone once famously remarked that he could think of no situation where having money didn't make it better. I can say the same thing about having a prototype. However, if it's clear on its face how it's made and how it works, then a prototype isn't necessary and terrific looking drawings will do the job instead. However, if your product is supposed to do something or accomplish some specific result, and if how that comes about isn't absolutely clear, then it's imperative that you have a working prototype that proves your idea will deliver what you promised it will. The prospective licensee is not going to invest his resources until he has something in his hands to see, use, and determine for himself its commercial viability. Without a prototype, there's doubt, and when doubt enters the room by one door, the licensing contract exits by another. If you're not prepared to prove that your product works, then you're wasting the executive's time and he or she is going to start gazing out of the window, hoping you'll leave soon.

Quite possibly you won't have the skill or tools to make a decent prototype yourself and may have to hire someone to do it for you. If this is the case, remember to first have him sign a nondisclosure agreement before disclosing the information about your product (there's a sample form in the Appendix). Even if this person's contribution is substantial, as discussed, don't make him a partner in the patent. If you're unable to make the prototype either because you don't have the expertise or equipment, there are plenty of talented model makers who can do the job for you; a simple Google search will give you lots of names and contact information. What I've found is that the local university is a good place to find help. With the help of the department head, you can perhaps find a bright, talented student who can create the prototype for you. Of course you'd be expected to pay him, but it would probably be much less than what a professional would charge. I taught product design at an art college where we had a well-equipped model shop. It was not uncommon for inventors and others to come by to hire a student for a project.

In addition to the prototype and any drawings or photos, there may be some written material that you'll need to help with your presentation and to leave with the executive. Sometimes, if the stars are in perfect alignment, the executive might be so excited about your proposed product that he'll want to make a deal on the spot. More likely, he'll ask that you call him back, perhaps in a week, giving him time to discuss the idea with his colleagues. It'll help your cause if you can leave him a report with pertinent information to help him present your idea effectively.

The more successfully the material you place into the prospect's hands can suggest the inevitable realization of your product idea (if not by this prospect then surely by a competitor), the easier it will be to close the deal. The message your material should convey is that your product *will* be in stores all over—it's just a matter of which company will put it there.

What I mean is, present your material like this:

1. Here's a picture showing what my product will look like when it's produced.

2. Here's a prototype that shows how my product will work when it's produced.

3. Here's a mock-up to show how my product will be packaged when it's produced.

4. Here's a drawing showing how the product will be displayed in stores.

Here's a tip about organizing your material. A number of years ago (before laptops) a friend of mine, an instructor at Temple University, asked if I could teach a marketing class for him because he had to be away. I was quite young (younger than some of the students), and having never done this before, I was quite nervous and probably overprepared. As I stood in front of the classroom of about 75 students, talking and talking, I had the uneasy sense that few in the room were paying attention. Heads drooped, eyes wandered, some couldn't stop fidgeting. Nevertheless, since fleeing was out of the question, I droned on and on until I happened to say something like, "Here are the six important things to remember about marketing a luxury product . . . " Suddenly a great rustling sound filled the room as everyone sat up in their seats and threw open their notebooks with pencils poised, ready to write down the gems of wisdom that were about to pour from my lips. I discovered what I guess every teacher in the world already knew: the magic of lists!

When you write your presentation, make it as brief as possible. And second, whenever information can be conveyed in list form, that's how to do it. Everybody loves lists! Smart people love lists, as do foolish people and rich people and poor people and big people and little people. Everybody who reads for information loves lists for the following five reasons:

1. Lists are easy to read.

2. Lists seem efficient.

3. Lists seem factual.

4. Lists seem to be to the point.

5. Lists seem conclusive.

All executives have the same peeve; they hate to have their time wasted. If what your handing your guy looks like bunch of hyperbole about how your Aunt Jennie loved this idea and how the guys at the firehouse think it's the best thing they ever saw, he'll just toss it aside, but if the report crisply presents the crucial material in a form something like this, it will earn his attention:

- Here are five ways that this product is better than the competitors.

- Here are four reasons why this product will replace the competition in the marketplace.

- Here are the three reasons why consumers will buy this product.

Your Aunt Jennie and the guys at the firehouse might be wonderful people, but they have no place in your presentation. You have to assume that the executive you're meeting with has a reasonable amount of intelligence or he wouldn't have the corner office, so you should present your material in the manner he expects to see it—brief, pertinent, factual, and to the point. Do that and he'll appreciate your professionalism. "No home will be without one!" is not what I mean by factual.

If the product idea you're presenting is for a consumer product, something to be sold in stores, then it's *really* important to show it to the prospective licensee in the way that the consumer might see it. Little will interest him more. What I'm talking about is a mock-up consumer package that demonstrates how convincingly your packaged product will sell itself in the kind of clerkless retail environment we've become accustomed to.

I can't stress too much how important this is, and I can only hope you'll take my word for it. If you can show the licensee how effectively and persuasively this product can present itself in a retail environment, not only have you won the battle, you've probably won the whole darned war. We're now on the licensee's turf—packaging, promotion, store displays—and when the conversation moves to those topics, you will have moved your idea out of the never-never land of product ideas to the realities of the marketplace, which is precisely where you want to be. We live in a self-service world, and the licensee wants to be sure that this product in its package will present a powerful reason to buy from a consumer wandering down a crowded aisle in some big store. The closer you bring him to the acceptance that you're presenting an exciting, salable product, the closer you'll be to making your own sale. You'll probably have to pay a graphic designer to make a dynamite package for you, but believe me, it's money well spent. I've seen lots of perfectly decent product ideas get abandoned in new product meetings because they couldn't be packaged in a logical way to explain and sell the product while it's sitting there on the retailer's shelf. Allay that fear and you're rounding third.

Incidentally, no matter how brilliant your mock-up package is, I can guarantee that's not the package that will wind up being used. The company's design department will feel that using an outsider's design is a challenge to their worth to the company, and they will redo it in their own way, perhaps not even as good as the mock-up. That's just the way these things work in these companies where everyone has turf to protect, but the important thing is that it was your package that landed the contract.

PREPARING YOUR GAME SHOW OR REALITY SHOW IDEA

The late Merv Griffin dreamed up two game shows, *Jeopardy* and *Wheel of Fortune,* allowing him to live his years like a potentate with riches to spare. While it's not likely for that to happen to you or me, that doesn't mean it's impossible. There are more than a hundred TV networks in operation, and all of them need content. If you have something brilliant that they can use, they'll happily make you a deal. I don't mean you personally since they probably won't see you; but it's possible that you can make a deal with the production company that they will see, and so indirectly the offer is being made to you. In any event, you and I both know what a long shot it is, but what the heck, why not give it a go? Your total investment is words on paper and the zeal to find someone in the business willing to hear what you've got.

But first things first: You have to prepare your idea in the way that the prospective TV producer wants to see it. Your essential material for your idea is what's called a "treatment." A treatment is not a script and it's not about camera angles. That's not your job. A treatment is a synopsis of what the show will be about in simple, straightforward language and needn't be more than a few double-spaced pages long. If your idea is for a reality show, you will describe the premise, suggest the location, the number of participants, and the job of the host. You will lay out a typical episode and explain the dramatic arc of the show—meaning what the quest will be, what incidents or episodes will eliminate members, what the rewards are, and how it all ends.

And then you need is a great name for your show, whether it's a game show or a reality show, and you need what's called a "log line." A log line is a pithy sentence or two that succinctly describes the essence of the idea and whets the appetite of the listener or reader to want to know more. Think of it like a coming attractions ad.

For example, here's what could have been the log line for *The Bachelor*, suggested by the TV Writers Vault (TVWritersVault.com): "Twenty women will court and compete to win the affections of one man who will narrow the selection until he must decide on his one true love."

Getting the log line just right is important—it's perhaps all that the busy executive will read and perhaps the make-or-break moment for the whole idea—so be prepared to give it the time it needs.

PREPARING YOUR INTERNET BUSINESS IDEA

Since, as discussed, you need to have something unique and proprietary to offer to the potential licensee to persuade him to sign a licensing deal for your Internet business idea, whatever that something special is must be available for him to see and confirm. You can't expect even your rich Uncle Louie to move ahead on blind trust, love you though he may. I assure you, he'll be guided by the old advice to trust everyone, but cut the cards.

If you've created a unique software program that will enable the licensee to process orders cheaper and faster or somehow give him an edge over the competition, you have to show him the software in action. If you have a strong domain name and a powerful website layout and a prime position on the search engines, you have to show him all of that as well. It's not difficult to make a dummy website for him to see. And if you have special access to the product that the website will sell, he'll want to see confirmation of that fact; or if you've invented a device or machinery to produce a unique product to sell that will be the basis for the company, he'll want to see it in action.

For example, I know someone who has invented and patented a device to take someone's portrait photo and turn it into a three dimensional charm or pendant. If he wanted to use his invention as the basis for licensing an Internet business idea, the prospective licensee would, of course, expect to see this device in action so he can determine if it works fast enough and cheaply enough to make the idea viable, and if the end result will please the customer.

In addition to this singular advantage that you're hoping will sway the deal, you have to give the prospective licensee a reason to be interested in this business in any event, which means a business plan. Your plan should offer an overview of the market situation, what the competitors are offering, why your licensee can gain a profitable share of the business, what expenses it will take to run and promote the site, what would be the investment in inventory, what could the product(s) or service sell for, what the profit margin would be, and of course, what profit returns can be expected. Turn the venture around and assume someone was coming to you with an Internet business idea instead of you going to them. Make a list of all the things you'd want to know before investing your money, and you can be sure your potential licensee will want to know all of that and more.

PREPARING YOUR SOFTWARE IDEA

It's not impossible for someone to sign a licensing deal with you simply for suggesting the idea, but it would be quite difficult. If you were already famous and accomplished in that field, the deal might be struck. The company might pay you to develop the program, considering the money given to you to be an advance against future royalty payments. However, that kind of deal is unlikely if you don't have the credentials to back it up.

That kind of arrangement would be more likely if you had a prototype for the manufacturer to see the nature of the program and how it would work. There are horizontal prototypes that give an overview of the entire program and vertical prototypes that take one step from beginning to end. If you're the developer, you'd know best which presents the concept more effectively. Words alone usually won't close the deal unless you have a reputation that precedes you.

In the end, however, the value is in the software itself, and nothing is as good as being able to show the prospective licensee a fully developed program that does what it's expected to do in an efficient manner and that answers an obvious need. Your prospective licensee is probably a company making or licensing and selling other software programs to the same type of audience that your program is directed to. If they're impressed with what you've accomplished, they will take your program, put it in one of their packages, market it directly to end users or through retailers (depending on the nature of the program), and pay you a royalty for each program sold.

Creating a software program, even a simple one, involves a tremendous investment in time and money, and so unless you were able to have already receive a commitment from a licensee, you will have to satisfy yourself that proceeding makes sense. Why should such a program exist? Who will buy it? What would they expect to pay for it? How many buyers might there be? In what important ways will this program be superior to existing ones? Can these potential customers easily be reached? Just as you had to be satisfied with the answers before committing to creating the software, so would the manufacturer need to be satisfied before making the licensing deal. He wants to know just what you wanted to know.

If you are not going to create the software yourself, but intend to hire a development company to do the job, the developer will undoubtedly offer a contract. Following are typical terms of such contacts.

The Services and the Scope of the Work

You will be expected to provide in written detail what information you will be providing to the developer and what the program, as developed, will accomplish. Both parties agree in writing that they're talking about the same thing.

The developer will agree to create the program to perform in the manner that the two of you agreed upon.

Payment Amount and Method of Payment

The developer will either quote an exact fee to do the job or offer an estimate of man-hours required with the fee per hour. Either way, by exact quote or estimate, a sum will be arrived at which is typically paid in thirds: when the job is started, halfway through upon approval, and when the finished program is delivered.

Expiration, Extension, Termination

The developer promises delivery at a certain date, provisions are made for extensions if caused by additional client requests, and reasons that can cause termination of this agreement by either party are stated and agreed upon.

Sundry Clauses

The agreement will cover other matters such as the developer's agreement to maintain confidentiality, a statement that the client owns the work, how disputes are handled (usually by arbitration), and so on. The principal agreement, however, is as stated: what the work is, what portion is the client's responsibility, what portion is the developer's responsibility, what the cost is, when the job is to be delivered, and how the fees are to be paid.

I understand that many of you are brilliant at creating wonderful ideas, but would rather die than go knocking on doors to find a buyer for them. I really do understand that. But I'm not going to kid you—if you won't physically get yourself in front of the person who can say "yes," or find someone to do it for you, it's almost a certainty that the idea will never be heard. Forget letters, forget e-mails, and forget making a website and thinking you've done something—it's you and you alone who can make great things happen. I can't make you become a salesperson for your idea; all I can say is that it's really not as bad as you might think. If you do knock on doors, no one is going to shoot you and no one is going to hold your first child as ransom. In fact, for some of us it's really fun. Showing my wonderful new idea to a prospective licensee who hopes I have something great to show him is the part of this business that I enjoy the most. Try it; you might discover that you're a genius salesman! And that's precisely what we're going to find out in the next chapter.

5

LET'S START THE SHOW!

*In the modern world of business, it is
useless to be a creative, original thinker
unless you can also sell what you create.
Management cannot be expected
to recognize a good idea unless it's
presented to them by a good salesman.*
—David Ogilvy, advertising executive

There are two reasons why so many folks who dream up interesting ideas or inventions will do everything under the sun to avoid actually going out to sell what they've invented. First, they feel they don't know how to sell, won't do a good job, and will embarrass themselves or be taken advantage of. And second, they fear that if they show their product idea to a stranger at some company, it will be stolen from them. I'll address the second issue first.

Back in the late 1930s and early 1940s, second-tier movie studios like Universal-International and Republic made B movies, one after another, often with the same recurrent theme:

> The kindly, gray-haired inventor, toiling selflessly in his basement laboratory, finally discovers (A) an incredible new death ray military weapon; or (B) a secret device to turn camel dung into hard, brilliant diamonds; or (C) an amazing formula for curing hemorrhoids. Getting wind of the discovery, Otto Heimlich, the evil president of Trans-Global Megalith, sends henchmen into the inventor's lab to steal (A) the death ray, (B) the secret plans, or (C) the magic cure. The thugs are discovered, a tussle ensues, and the thugs take what they came for—leaving the kindly old inventor (A) dead, (B) unconscious, or (C) really, really mad.

> Grief-stricken, swearing vengeance, and hurling herself at the impenetrable gray walls of the vile conglomerate, is sweet, pretty Mary Wilson, who is either (A) the inventor's daughter, or (B) his niece, or (C) his ward. Then, suddenly, appears a brave soul who rushes to be at her side. He's either (A) the handsome, fearless detective; or (B) the handsome, fearless reporter; or (C) the handsome, fearless patent attorney.

I won't bore you with the rest of the saga except to say that some evil specter implanted this story into the genes of naïve, young, inventors-to-be where it became impossible to dislodge. Now, handed down from father to son, millions of inventors will swear that Otto Heimlich still exists, maneuvering to steal their discoveries and inventions. Never mind that poor Heimlich would now be over a hundred, needing a walker to keep lurking around. When some company executive innocently says to these inventors, "Tell me about your invention," you can see the panic flash in their eyes.

I try to combat this fear with sweet reasoning, but must confess I'm not always successful. I press on, however, using what I call the *Four Irrefutable Reasons Why a Company Will Not Steal Your Idea.*

IRREFUTABLE REASON #1: WHY WOULD THE COMPANY INVITE A LAWSUIT?

As previously mentioned, the courts have usually ruled that if you show your secret idea to a company in good faith, they can't just steal it for their own benefit. You will have left a paper trail and you will have gotten at least a provisional patent on your idea. The company, in order to defend its crooked actions, would have to create fake documents and try to get employees to lie under oath. What company would engage in such a high-risk game when it's so easy to just make a deal for your idea in the first place?

IRREFUTABLE REASON #2: NO OFFENSE, BUT YOU CAN BE BOUGHT CHEAP

To a company hungering for your new product or invention, you're the biggest bargain to come down the pike in years. For about a 5 percent royalty and a little upfront money, they can close the deal. For every dollar that comes into their till, they get 95 cents and you get a nickel. That's just like stealing, except it's legal.

IRREFUTABLE REASON #3: WHY CHASE YOU AWAY (MAYBE YOU WON'T COME BACK)?

If you show your new product idea to Company A, and if the representative lies, telling you that it's an idea the company is already working on—won't you just go across the street and give it to the competitors? For a measly royalty the company keeps you from walking away and gets to keep the idea. Further, if you suspect the person is lying, you won't come back to that company with your next idea. This first idea might be okay, but the next idea might be sensational. You're certainly not going to give it to Company A if you were treated shoddily before; you'll give it to Company B, Company

A's biggest competitor. No company chases away a person proven to bring fresh, original, profitable ideas.

I had a similar event happen to me; not the same but close. I showed my new product idea to a company and they showed me a prototype of a product they were working on that was virtually the same thing. Undaunted, I went across town and licensed my product to a competitor, even though honesty compelled me to say that I knew the first company was already working on something similar. In my instance the first company wasn't lying, but they could have been and I would have still gone to their competitor. Interestingly, my licensee came out with my version of the product, but the first company never came out with theirs. Maybe I was lucky after all.

IRREFUTABLE REASON #4: IT'S SIMPLY NOT GOOD BUSINESS, EVEN FOR HEIMLICH

The company might be made up entirely of the heirs of Otto Heimlich, crooked as they come, but if making a deal with you is so cheap and easy, it doesn't make good sense to try and steal your idea. Yes, they might bargain for a better deal; that's okay, that's business. The Heimlich gang might be rotten to the core, but trying to steal your idea is a stupid stunt, and no one said they're stupid. Even if the company's instincts are less than admirable, simple common sense and personal gain will keep them honest.

Companies aren't lurking to steal your invention.

Now, as far as being afraid because you won't know how to do it and will look stupid, I have some ready answers for that as well. First, if the product is really great and if your presentation material is fresh and engaging, you could be the bride of Frankenstein and the company will still be enthusiastic about making a deal with you. All that's required is for you to show up so they can see that you're a responsible-looking person and that they're not going to have any trouble in your ongoing mutual relationship.

"Yes," you might say, "but suppose they don't like my idea? What do I say then?" Because I don't consider myself to be an inventor, but instead consider myself to be in the inventing business, my life isn't wrapped around one idea or another and nothing that another person might say about the idea I'm peddling at the moment do I take personally; it's simply business. In fact, the word "inventing" is barely in my vocabulary. I'm a product developer; I create and sell product ideas. I figure if the guy doesn't like what I'm selling today, that doesn't mean that he won't like what I'm selling tomorrow. If you can adopt this attitude and not think of your idea as your baby, something so important and personal that any snub is an insult, you'll be able to shrug off any slings and arrows that might come your way.

And, please allow me to disabuse you of the notion that you can just send out some mailings and sit back waiting for the phone to ring. It won't; I can assure you. I've tried it myself and I know others who have tried it, with zero results. While I won't say it's absolutely, positively, 100 percent guaranteed to fail, I can say that I've personally never closed a deal from mailing something to someone at a company that I don't know and who doesn't know me, and I never met any inventor who did either—and I know lots of inventors. Selling product ideas is simply a face-to-face business. And besides, you will learn so much more of value when you meet personally with the prospective licensee than you could ever learn by a mail exchange, that I'm confident you'll agree that going postal makes no sense.

WHY YOU'LL LEAVE THE MEETING WITH A SMILE ON YOUR FACE

Let's say that you've met with the prospective licensee, made a brilliant presentation, and are now sitting back in your chair, awaiting his comments. Hopefully, he's going to jump up, give you a hug, and tell you what a brilliant idea this is. But suppose he doesn't? Even if he doesn't grab for his checkbook, he'll have one of four other opinions about your idea, which can also be to your benefit in a different way.

What Can Happen #1

Even if he says the idea isn't for him, the meeting will still have been valuable if you press for further clarification. What you want to know is if that's what he really means—that the product isn't right for his company—or is he really saying that he doesn't think much of the idea itself? If you're satisfied that he means the former, perhaps he can suggest who it might be for. Hopefully he can be prompted to say something like, "Well, while I'm sure this wouldn't fit into our business, it might be something that Amalgamated would be interested in. Show it to Hank Gordon over there and tell him that Bill Franconi said, 'Hi.'" With that, getting an appointment with Amalgamated should be no problem. "Hello, Mr. Gordon? My name's Joe Smith. I'm calling at the suggestion of Bill Franconi at Ajax who told me to say 'Hi' to you. He suggested I should call you because he thought you'd probably be interested in what I'd like to show you." You're not going to get leads like that from sending out a mailing.

What Can Happen #2

You might determine that Bill Franconi isn't just saying that the idea isn't for his company; he might really be saying that he doesn't like the idea itself, period. With a little encouragement he might be willing to offer some design changes that could make the product better, cheaper, faster, or whatever. By offering improvement suggestions, Franconi is taking ownership of the idea. When you call the next time, saying you want to show him the new, improved version based on his guidance, he'll say come right over.

What Can Happen #3

If Bill Franconi simply doesn't like the idea at all—period—with no improvements or suggestions to offer, maybe this product actually isn't as brilliant as you thought it was; maybe it really is a lousy idea. Isn't that worth knowing? If Franconi shows you the fatal flaw with your idea, you have to man up to it. Being realistic is what separates the amateur from the professional. Nobody is going to answer your letter and tell you this. If the company even bothers to answer at all, it'll simply be a polite, "No thanks."

What Can Happen #4

Okay, so you're convinced that Franconi thinks this idea stinks and is beyond redemption, so it's time to move on. But wait a minute: You're in his office, chatting away, so what could be more logical than to ask what kind of product he is looking for? He might say something like, "Well, I'm sorry I don't like this idea, but if you could bring me something that does *this* or *that*, then I might really be interested." The best inventors uncover the need before inventing, and then invent to fill the need. That sounds so logical when I write it, but you'd be amazed how many inventors do it the other way around. By Franconi identifying a need—a target for your creativity— this rejection meeting might pay for itself many times over. A potential licensee telling you what to invent for him could be a goldmine. None of this would take place for the inventor who just sends out a mailing and waits for the checks to appear in his mailbox. Inventing-for-profit is a business, and it has to be approached as such. Contacts are valuable and you just made a good one.

MINING FOR PROSPECTS FOR YOUR PRODUCT INVENTION

First you have to decide if you're going to handle this yourself or try to gain the services of an agent. Even though I'm an agent myself, as you know, the entire thrust of this book is to show you how to do it yourself and why you should do it yourself. Yes, maybe I can do it for you, but I believe you can probably do it better. In most instances, agents like myself should be Plan B—to use (if you can get one) when, for any number of reasons, you're unable to knock on doors on your own or if your product idea is for a field where agents dominate.

For instance, I write books. I need an agent; or at least I did need one when I was first starting out and was unknown. Most publishers won't deal directly with writers, and if you send them an unsolicited manuscript, it will wind up in a slush pile, eventually looked at (if at all) by some unpaid intern with nothing else to do. Similarly, if you have an idea for a TV show, which we'll discuss later, networks won't see you, but if you have an agent they know and trust, they'll see him or her. There are other fields where you need an agent. The big game companies, like Parker Brothers, or the big toy companies, like Milton Bradley, deal only with agents. In any field where the number of people wanting to sell an idea grossly outnumbers those looking to buy one, agents are used because they're professionals who have screened the ideas, culled out the decent ones, and won't be wasting the executive's time. If you have invented a new wheelbarrow, you don't need an agent. The waiting room of any wheelbarrow company is not exactly crowded with people who have new wheelbarrow inventions to show them, and so an agent has no better access than you would.

Benjamin Disraeli once said, "It is well known what an agent is. An agent is a man who bamboozles one party and plunders another." My definition is not as witty, but I believe more accurate. My definition of an agent is a salesperson who has access to decision makers, who will represent the inventor's interest to them, and whose remuneration is a percentage of the money earned by this effort. By all counts, invention promotion companies don't meet this definition. They have no more access to decision makers than the man in the moon, they clearly don't have the inventor's best interests at heart, and while they make claims about participating in royalties, they really make their money through the large fees that they charge.

If you call an invention promotion company and ask them to be your agent, you'll receive a resounding "Yes!" with the instructions to get out your checkbook. However, if you call a legitimate agent (assuming he takes your call), the response will usually be a negative one. Since agents spend their own money and depend upon success for their rewards, they are understandably highly selective. However, this is a very subjective business with no one positively knowing whether an idea is good or not. Any agent in any field can tell you of ideas they turned down that went on to be hugely successful. It's just the nature of this business. J. K. Rowling, the author of the Harry Potter books, was turned down by a whole slew of agents before one took her on—and even then, all the large publishers turned down the manuscript. Finally a small house agreed to be the publisher.

YOUR DEAL WITH THE AGENT

If you do find an agent who appreciates the brilliance of your idea, you'll have to sign a standard agency agreement. These contracts are short and not complicated, and I'm confident that you'll comprehend the points covered without the need to pay a lawyer.

A copy of my own agency agreement is in the Appendix. As you'll see, it covers the following points and is typical of other agency agreements I have seen.

1. Commissions

    Commissions for the agent usually range from 10 percent to 50 percent, depending on the level of the agent's contribution and what he has to invest in prototypes and presentation material to bring the proposed product up to a professional level. Commission payments might be for a specified time or for as long as the property is earning income. Almost always it's the latter.

2. Exclusivity Period

    This clause pertains to how long the agreement will be in force. Since the agent is usually appointed on an exclusive basis, the agreement cannot be in perpetuity (my own is for six months). At some point, if nothing is happening, the agreement expires and the parties can go their own ways, owing each other nothing. As a practical matter, the agent usually knows in a month or two whether he's going to be successful and would have no reason to want to see the agreement drag on. He will usually resign before being fired.

3. Out-of-Pocket Expenses

    This clause delineates agreed-upon charges that will be billed to the inventor, if any. Depending on the situation, the inventor might have agreed to split or fully pay the costs for the prototype or special presentation material. Who pays what is spelled out in this clause.

4. Method of Payment

    This refers to the process of splitting the royalty proceeds. Customarily the licensee remits payment and the sales report to the agent, who deposits the check and uses his own check to send the inventor his share along with a copy of the licensee's report. I've never seen a contract that was the other way around.

5. Cancellation

    And finally, the agreement spells out the rights and obligations of the parties should the agreement be terminated without a successful outcome. Client-agent relations in most fields can be volatile and frequently don't last too long, and by mutual agreement, the parties might end the arrangement before the termination date. The client feels that the agent isn't spending the time needed to look for a deal, and the agent might think that his client has become a pest and that he made a mistake taking on the product in the first place. When or if the breakup occurs, the agent agrees to continue to maintain confidentiality and can't use the idea or invention for his own purposes. However, within a specified period, say six months, if any of the companies that were originally contacted by the agent decides to go ahead with a licensing deal (even if the inventor personally made subsequent contacts), the agent gets his share.

To find out if agents are active in the field that you're interested in, a good place to look is the "Who Makes It" website directory for your particular industry. Almost every industry has a website like that, usually managed by the industry trade association or principal trade magazine in that field. Typically all the member companies are listed, followed by the suppliers to these companies. If there are agents, that's usually where they'd be found, in the supplier section. Also, if you belong to a local inventors club, asking fellow members about agents might bring a whole host of recommendations (including who to stay away from).

One More Thing About Agents

Assuming the principal reason for you looking for an agent is not to avoid doing the selling yourself, but because of the agent's access to decision makers, then you shouldn't confine your search to the roster of professional agents. Access to decision makers can come from many different sources. Anyone can be your agent, even the guy who does your dry cleaning, if that person provides what you're looking for. Your golfing buddy might have a cousin who's an executive at the perfect company for your idea, or your lawyer or accountant might have a client looking for what you're selling. Ask around; don't be shy. Network. Ask your friends on Facebook. I spend a lot of time in Asia working on products for clients where everyone's second career is as an agent. Introductions are bought and sold all the time. It's the same thing in Washington. Access to lawmakers or those responsible for making procurement decisions has made millionaires of more than one retired senator or admiral.

Continuing the earlier assumption that your invention was for a new type of wheelbarrow, the logical licensee would come from the ranks of the companies that already make wheelbarrows or hand trucks or dollies or carts of one sort or another. It's not likely that you'll interest a company not already in the same or an allied field, and so creating the prospect list is simple. All sorts of directories, such as the Thomas Register, can identify these companies.

If I was prioritizing my prospect list, all other things being equal, I'd put at the top the companies that I can easily get to because I'd want to put my idea personally into the hands of the person running the company. If I had other choices I'd of course prefer a company that sells lots of wheelbarrows—maybe not the top dog but the one right beneath. The assumption is that being second might make management a bit more receptive to new ideas than the fat and contented company on top. In reality, that might be true or not true—but it sounds logical so why not? It's as good a theory as any.

The Magic of Trade Shows

Another valuable asset in selecting and connecting with a potential licensee is to attend the trade show where your likely prospects will be exhibiting. If your wheelbarrow idea is for the kind of wheelbarrow a home gardener might use, then you'd look for a show where those types of manufacturers exhibit. That would probably be the National Hardware Show in Las Vegas. Or, if you application is industrial, there are all sorts of industrial equipment shows for you to select from.

If you attend the right show, in a couple of days you can introduce your idea to every company in the industry that might conceivably have an interest. Walk into the booth and tell whoever approaches you that you're an inventor (product developer) with a new product idea and ask who you should talk to. You'll either meet the right person you need on the spot, or you'll have a name and an introduction to follow up with. "Hello, Mr. Smith. I had a chat with Jeff Hawkins (he's the sales manager) in your booth at the recent Industrial Show and showed him the new wheelbarrow product I just invented. He thought you'd be very interested and suggested I contact you for an appointment." And so on.

A simple Google or Bing search can name sites that will tell of the dates and purpose of trade shows all around the world. Here are a few of them:

www.biztradeshows.com

www.eventseye.com

www.EventsinAmerica.com

www.MyTradeFairs.com

MINING FOR PROSPECTS FOR YOUR NEW TV SHOW IDEA

If you invented a great new wheelbarrow, as discussed, the companies that might be interested in a product like this can be easily identified and you can almost certainly get an audience to show what you've invented. The number of folks in the United States who are inventing new wheelbarrows can probably fit into my broom closet with room left over for two brooms. If you have a great new idea for a wheelbarrow company, the company will probably send a limo to pick you up at the airport.

However, unfortunately, there are a gazillion folks with new TV show ideas and nobody in the business is particularly interested in hearing about them. Most production companies won't see you, most TV networks won't see you, and most agents won't see you. If truth be told, they'd all rather that you just went away. Unless you live where the market is (New York or Los Angeles) and know somebody who knows somebody, or you're already in the industry and are hobnobbing with the right people at cocktail parties or industry events, then getting someone to even listen to your idea is really, really difficult. "An accountant from Kansas City with a game idea? Puh-lease! What could he possibly have to show us that might be interesting?" Sorry, nothing personal, but that's how it is.

The good news is that while, yes, it is really, *really* difficult to get an audience, that doesn't mean it's impossible. There are regular folks like us who do sell their TV show ideas, so the door isn't closed completely. There are some steps and strategies to take, and since so far your investment in your idea is zero, why not give it a shot? Here are some moves to consider:

Possibility #1: Networking

It's sad but true that if you live in Los Angeles or New York, you will probably have a much better chance of networking your way into a pitch meeting with the perfect agent or production company for your new game show or reality show idea. Since so many folks in those cities have jobs in or connected to the entertainment industry, there's a good chance that you'll know somebody who knows somebody who knows somebody.

All the experts in the business agree—nothing works better in getting a meeting than being able to say, "Joe sent me." For the rest of us it's not so easy, but not impossible. If you ask around, you might find that one of your mother's friend's friend has a son who made it big in Hollywood and now heads up the Ajax Production Company (just the folks you'd like to handle your idea). You could be pleasantly surprised at the connections that might exist by networking with everyone you know. At least try; it costs nothing.

Possibility #2: Bearding the Lion

Networking is easy and casual, taking no time to speak of; you just sort of do it as you go along. The next step, however, will take a lot of time, but the effort might pay off for you. It's not hard to find lists of agents, production companies, and TV networks on the Internet. I've listed a few sources below. Every agent, every production company, and every TV network has a website. If you visit the sites that are pertinent to your project, you'll probably find an executive's name (usually in the About Us section) and you'll probably find their policy about unsolicited submissions. Most organizations won't accept them, but a query letter is not an unsolicited submission— a query letter is simply a one-pager to tell the company that you have a wonderful new TV show idea and would like to submit the details. Give them the title and the log line (both of which you will have previously registered with the Writers Vault), and if the person reading your letter likes the idea, he'll request that you send him or her your treatment or synopsis. If you send out, say, 20 query letters, you might have invested about $10 in paper and stamps— and maybe it's money down the drain—but you can spend $10 for lunch and, who knows, maybe not all 20 responses will be rejections.

After reading your idea synopsis, if the company executive continues to like what he sees, he'll offer to pay you for an option to give the company time to present the idea to a network or two. Taking an option doesn't necessarily mean that the show will ever be produced, but there are folks who make a nice living just on options. More on that in the next chapter; for now here are some websites to start your search:

www.Boogar.com

www.WGA.Org

www.Hcdonline.com

www.TVWritersVault.com

Proactive Steps Requiring an Investment

So far it's been pretty much a free ride—some time and some postage stamps—but here are two proactive steps for you consider that will cost some money, but at least they should bring you some fast results (positive or negative).

The Television Writer's Vault (www.tvwritersvault.com) was started by a fellow named Scott Manville, who, for a number of years, was the head development executive for Merv Griffin Enterprises. Being in the trenches, so to speak, Manville recognized the problem of lots of TV show ideas floating around (some of them brilliant) with the creators being frustrated because they couldn't get an audience—and lots of agents and production company executives anxious to get their hands on a brilliant idea, but not willing to be bored to death by listening to endless pitches for bad ones, sort of like the princess needing to kiss so many frogs to find Prince Charming. What Manville did was figure out a fast, painless, inexpensive way for these entities to meet electronically without busting the bank and without trying anyone's time or patience.

The Writer's Vault has approximately 300 professional members— agents, network people, and production executives. For $39.95 (as of this writing), your TV show idea—the name, log line, and synopsis—will be posted in a members-only directory on the website for one month ($149 for six months). Hopefully, during that time a certain number of professional members will be cruising the directory to see what's new. If what you're offering catches the eye of one of these folks, the site has a method for that person to make contact, and the two of you would take it from there. I know for a fact that this is legitimate and that deals have been made through this process. Common sense would tell us that it's a long shot, but what the heck—this whole business is a crapshoot. If the investment isn't a burden, I think it's well worth considering.

Here's another interesting company whose services are worth a look. Virtual Pitch Fest (www.VirtualPitchFest.com) was started by David Zuckerman, a well-known industry professional, and while it's directed primarily at screenwriters, it can work for those with TV show ideas as well if approached judiciously. As with the Writers Vault, Virtual Pitch Fest also has hundreds of members, made up mainly of movie people and agents. However, if you visit "The Pros" page on their website, it lists the production companies and agents who are members and states what genres they're looking for. While, as I say, most are seeking movie scripts, there are enough production companies and agents who are open to TV ideas to make this a potentially viable option.

Here's the deal: For $50 (as of this writing) the Virtual Pitch Fest will e-mail your pitch material to five target executives of your choosing and guarantees a response from each of these executives within five days. For $90 they'll do the same thing for 10 target companies. While admittedly a long shot, the virtue of this program is that at least you'll know that somebody of some importance in the industry, a production company executive or agent, has actually read your proposal and actively responded with an expression of interest or no interest. That has to be worth something.

For less than a hundred dollars you can try both programs and at least have a sense that you made an active effort to get your TV idea seen and responded to. Maybe something good will come of it and maybe not. Is it worth the gamble? That's up to you.

MINING FOR PROSPECTS FOR YOUR NEW SOFTWARE PROGRAM

Since the production of a disk holding a software program is quite inexpensive, and since the creation of the program itself can be very expensive, most individuals who invest in software programs do so with the intention of marketing it themselves for the full profit— either directly to end users or through a network of distributors. They are, in all respects, in the software business. However, since we are meeting here on this page, I assume your goal is to produce the software, turn it over to a company to market, receive a smaller portion of the ongoing profits, and go back to your daytime career as a brain surgeon or astronaut or a taxidermist or whatever. That makes mining for prospects a whole lot easier.

If you do a Google, Yahoo!, or Bing search, you'll find directories of software companies in a particular industry or specialty (graphics, chemistry, automotive, business management, and so on), or if you go to general directories like www.Programplaz.com, or www .soft411.org (or similar sites), you can find just about every software company in business, thousands of them, categorized by their specialty or industry. A careful search should provide you with a list of companies that would be a perfect partner for your own program. From that point, as we discuss in the next chapter, it's as simple as picking up the phone.

IS THERE AN APP FOR THIS?

When folks tell me they have a new software idea it's usually at the app level rather than some sophisticated, highly intricate software program taking hundreds of hours and many thousands of dollars to develop. If you had an app idea—for instance, let's say it's for fantasy baseball players—and if you took that idea to one of the people running a fantasy baseball website, you might conceivably be able to strike a deal with them. However, your chances would be enormously better if the app was already developed so they could see how it works and what it does. If the program was fully developed and tested, and if it was really clever, I think you could find a licensee for it without difficulty.

Most app owners don't make money from their apps, nor do they expect to. Most apps are developed by companies that have other goods or services to sell, and so the app is really an introduction to who they are and what they do. I don't mean that the apps don't provide a valuable service unto themselves; most do. But since they're usually free or sell for a few dollars, it's clearly not app profits that most of these owners are after. So, if you can put a fully developed fantasy baseball app into the hands of one of these website owners—an app that they could market under their own name to promote their website—I think licensing would just be a matter of working out the details.

MINING FOR PROSPECTS FOR YOUR INTERNET BUSINESS IDEA

Country clubs all over America are filled with guys who sold their business, made some money, retired early, and are now playing gin and golf and are generally bored to tears. Lots of these entrepreneurial types might be interested in having a unique website business proposition idea handed to them; it's just the kind of opportunity they've been looking for—something that they can maybe do part time and still be available for an occasional gin game with the boys or a round or two of golf. Picturing these guys is easy, but getting your idea in front of a couple of them might take a bit of doing.

As is so often the case, networking can be the easiest answer to the problem. You might not personally know of any well-off early retirees looking for some action, but I'll bet some of your friends or relatives do. You only have to meet one of them. Show him your idea and he might become interested himself (or maybe he'll be interested for his son or daughter or wife) or, more than likely, he'll put you in touch with one of his gin buddies who's looking for just what you're offering. "Here's a number; the guy's name is Max. Tell him I said for you to call." Also, speak to the usual suspects like your lawyer or accountant; they might easily have a client or two who fits description of the kind of chap you're looking for. Networking is Plan A because it's free and so often works. Everything else is Plan B.

One of the Plan B options, assuming you live in or near a large city, is to call on one of the local business brokers. They sell businesses— you have a business for sale (or to license)—so maybe you can do each other some good. Lots of these brokers also sell franchise deals, so your own business is not too far removed from their areas of expertise.

The main thing they have to offer is that men and women come to them with the desire to buy a business, so it's not inconceivable that your own business idea might suit them just fine. Business brokers work on commission, so it might at least be worth a conversation.

If your proposed Internet business is terrific, they can possibly find you a customer. After all, connecting buyers with sellers is precisely what they do.

There's another Plan B that's worth your consideration. Just as there are local, conventional business brokers as we just discussed, there are also national business brokers who specialize in selling Internet businesses. Following are the sites for a few of them. While yes, yours is not yet a going business, and while, yes, you're looking for a licensing deal not an outright sale, what you are offering *is* a business on the Internet, so a telephone call or two might lead to surprising results. Some sites to explore follow, but meanwhile, don't stop networking.

www.websiteproperties.com

www.businessmart.com

www.businessnation.com

www.quietlightbrokerage.com

Regardless of the nature of your new idea or invention, there's somebody who wants to hear about it and shower you with riches (assuming, of course, that it's brilliant). Now that you have identified who that lucky someone is, at least by title and organization, how do you land an appointment with him (and what do you say when we get it)? All will be revealed in the next chapter.

You can't make a score if you don't have a goal.

6

What to Say and How to Play

Landing the Perfect Appointment with the Perfect Person at the Perfect Company

The secret of success in life is for a man to be ready for his opportunity when it comes.

—Benjamin Disraeli

If someone from Upper Snowshoe, South Dakota, wanted to get into the business I'm in—creating product ideas for a living—I would advise him or her to take a map and draw a circle around Upper Snowshoe, 100 miles in all directions. And then I'd suggest that this person make a list of every company within this circle—of course not including pizza parlors, dry cleaners, and places like that—and then I'd tell this person to focus his or her creative energies on creating products only for those companies. The 100 miles is arbitrary, but I figure that it's still close enough to be able to drop in on a company in a casual manner and build a relationship with management. The inventor will learn what kind of products the company is looking for and will invent to their needs. If this inventor from Upper Snowshoe can strike up this kind of association with maybe a half dozen companies within the magic circle, he or she will be busy all the time and the income will grow. I'm taking for granted that this person has the creativity to do the job—my contribution is to urge him or her to use that creativity with companies that are close by because it's the personal visits that will make everything happen. Management in these companies will get to know the person and be comfortable dealing with him, and because the inventor will get to know the company, the ideas will be highly focused and will almost always be what the company is looking for.

There are two things I know in this business: The first is that nothing will happen with your idea until you take it under your arm and go out to meet the world; and the second is that if you show your idea to clerks, assistants, and underlings, they will waste your time and break your heart. You have to get yourself in front of the decision maker if you want a decision to be made. That's how these folks earn their living—by making decisions. Spending your time with underlings who can say "no" but don't have the authority to say "yes" is not only a waste of time, it's a heartbreaker. It doesn't matter what you're selling—a product invention or a software program on a game show—if you deal with underlings your idea will die with them.

The marketing assistants, design department employees, and engineers who you might think are the logical folks in the company to first show your idea to are precisely the people you want to avoid. These folks are your enemies, so recognize them for what they are. It is their job to come up with tweaks, design changes, and improvements for the company's products, and so when you come out of left field with some wonderful new product idea that perhaps they should have thought of themselves, they see you as a threat and believe it is not in their best interest to allow you to succeed. These folks will listen and smile and ask intelligent questions and string you along forever, but bumping the idea up to the boss is the last thing on their minds. This attitude among second-tier employees against outsiders with product ideas is so prevalent and known that it actually has a name: the N.I.H. Syndrome—"Not Invented Here." If the idea comes from some dumb outsider it can't possibly be as good as the ideas that are generated by these insider folks themselves. They live in fear that the boss will say, "Hey, why didn't you think of this idea?"

Fortunately for us, their boss—the department head for a larger company or the president for a smaller one—couldn't care less where a good idea comes from. He wants profits for his company because that's how he's rewarded, so you could be Vlad the Impaler or Attila the Hun but, if you have a profit making idea, he'll say, "Come right in, Mr. Attila, and have a seat."

This is where the fun part comes in. In just the briefest of telephone calls, you have to convince some tough, high-powered executive to take time out of his or her busy day to see you. Will they laugh? Will they slam the phone down? Will they tell you to go fly a kite? You can relax. In most situations, getting an appointment with this person is a lot easier than you think. You just have to know what to say and how to play. Yes, you might have to stretch the truth a little bit (but in a harmless way) and have a little nerve, but the possible rewards so far outweigh any momentary mental discomfort that it's hardly worth thinking about. Just follow these simple, foolproof instructions.

Four Things to Remember When You Call for an Appointment

1. *Do not present yourself as an amateur*. You have to accept the fact that companies do not want to deal with amateur inventors. First, because they doubt that the amateur has anything worthwhile to show them and will waste their time, and second because of the belief that amateurs tend to think that everyone from the housekeeper emptying the wastebaskets to the receptionist in the lobby to the clerk in the next cubbyhole are all plotting and scheming to steal their new idea. That might be a bum

rap, but inventors do have a reputation of being a bit, shall we say, *eccentric.* That's one of the reasons that the word "inventor" is barely in my vocabulary. I identify myself as a product developer because it is how I think of myself and because it has a more professional sound to it. If an executive will think twice about inviting an inventor into his office, he won't feel that way about a professional product developer.

I can tell you that when inventors call to ask to show me their ideas personally, I always respectfully decline. The first reason why I decline is that I've found that once the inventor's in my office, it's difficult to get him to leave; the second reason is because so many inventors take their idea personally, so when I tell them I don't like it, they're ready for a fight, insisting that I just don't understand the idea. If I wasn't so stupid and pig-headed and really understood it, they say, I'd love it. To them this idea is their baby—and you don't tell a mother that her baby is ugly. A professional doesn't take personal possession of a product idea, and if the executive tells him he doesn't like it, he doesn't go ballistic—he just tries to find out why so he can know what to do next—either fix it or abandon it and move on.

Since we know that companies prefer to deal with professionals, because professionals are businesspeople just as they are and are more likely to have something worthwhile to show (which they do quickly), then that's what you should become on the telephone. Consider yourself at war, and the first casualty of war is truth. You're not going to call the Green Velvet Mower Company and tell the person on the other end of the line that you're a cashier at a local Walgreens and have a cute idea for their lawnmowers. How far do you think that approach will get you? By innuendo you're going to present yourself as a successful professional, and I'll tell you how in just a moment.

2. *Go for the president.* If the company is small- or medium-sized, regardless of all the titles, it's really the president/owner who calls the shots, so he is your target. If it's a large company, trying to reach the president will probably be futile—and that's not who you want anyway. If you've invented a new kind of bandage that you'd like to show to Johnson & Johnson, you want the person in charge of the bandages division. Someone in that huge company makes the decisions about bandages, and that's who you want—who you don't want is some third-level assistant who promises to show your invention to the boss (who is away on vacation at the moment). Nothing good can come from that. Call one day and get the name of the division

head from some operator and then call the next day and ask for your old pal Bill Duffy. It really can be that simple.

3. *Keep the conversation brief.* When you get Bill Duffy on the phone, keep your conversation as brisk and brief as possible, short of being rude. Remember that the purpose of your call is to get an appointment. When you get it, say thank you, and hang up. If you linger on the telephone chatting with Duffy, you might say too much and the appointment might get cancelled right before your eyes.

    Duffy will find out that you're a cashier at a local Walgreens, and you'll give him a scrap of information about the idea and that can be the killer. "Okay. I get it. I don't want to waste your time with an appointment. How about you just send me some information and we'll let you know if we want to pursue it further." As someone named Olin Miller once said, "When a person says he'll let you know—you know." Those are the words you don't want to hear, and so you have to get out of Dodge before they can be said.

    Think of yourself as a commando on a mission (to get an appointment). Once the mission has been accomplished and the bombs have been planted, you have to get out of there as quickly as possible. If you hang around to admire the explosions, you'll probably be a goner. Any surviving commando will tell you that.

4. *Niceness pays.* It is so obvious that folks are inclined to be more helpful if they're approached in a warm, pleasant, friendly way that I have to wonder why so many folks present themselves in a rude, abrupt, and arbitrary manner. If you're impatient with the person at the other end of the phone, treating him or her as some sort of underling, you might find yourself at the receiving end of some payback that you won't like. If you're in the boss's office, showing him, say, your new doggie-pooper-scooper idea, he's apt to call in his assistant. "Jane, I know you keep your two dogs in a fenced-off area at home—so what do you think of this pooper-scooper idea?" If you were rude to Jane the other day on the phone, what do you think she might say?

THE MAGIC TWO-MINUTE TELEPHONE APPOINTMENT-GETTER CONVERSATION

The following script has appeared in earlier editions of this book, and over the years I've heard from so many inventors who have tried it and told me how great it works that I'm repeating it here. It's a short, one-act play called *The Appointment*.

THE CAST

HELEN FURY, Receptionist

HECTOR GREENBOTTOM, Vice President

MAX DUBOIS, President Global Amalgamated Things

BUSTER BALDWIN, Greenbottom's assistant

DONNA MADONNA, Max Dubois' assistant

THOMAS ALVA REDDISON, Dashing young inventor

FURY:	Hello Global—can you hold? (*Good. A busy receptionist doesn't have time for questions.*)
FURY:	(*moments later*) Hello—sorry to keep you waiting.
REDDISON:	That's okay, let me have Max Dubois please.
	(*Reddison will have called a few days earlier to get the president's name from the operator, who will have long forgotten that earlier call when you asked, "I have to send a letter to your president, can I have his name please?" Or perhaps Dubois' name was on the company website.*)
FURY:	Ringing.
MADONNA:	Hello, Mr. Dubois' office.
REDDISON:	Hi. My name's Tom Reddison. We create new products for companies and have come up with something that I know Max will want to see—so if you could just put me through, I'd appreciate it. (*Spoken in a warm, friendly, conversational voice. Saying "Max," not "Mr. Dubois," suggests an established relationship. Note that Reddison always says "we," not "I."*)
MADONNA:	One moment.
DUBOIS:	(*in a rushed voice*) Dubois here!
REDDISON:	Hi, Mr. Dubois. My name's Tom Reddison. Thanks for taking the call. I'll only take a second—I know you're busy. We design new products for companies and our research led us to develop a wonderful new product that I know would be perfect for Global. I know your product line quite well and wouldn't call if I didn't think

this was a perfect match. If I could have a few moments to show it to you, I promise you won't be disappointed.

Note how this took about 15 seconds and covered all the bases:

A. You thanked Dubois and assured him of brevity, promising him that you're not a time-waster.

B. You suggested yourself to be the principal of a product design company, not a lone inventor. And note the magic word: "research."

C. Stating your familiarity with Global's product line suggests that you've done your homework and have something appropriate to discuss. Assuring Dubois that he'll like it shows confidence in yourself and in the idea.

D. Promising a short get-together allays Dubois' fears of a time-wasting meeting (the one thing all executives detest).

At this point Dubois will respond in one of three ways:

1. Okay, when do you want to come in?

2. Sounds interesting—what have you got?

3. Oh, you want my partner, Hector Greenbottom. He handles all new products. *(Whatever his response, you can be sure that Dubois will not tell you to go away because the company is not interested in any great new products.)*

If Dubois' answer is number 1 ("When do you want to come in?"), Reddison makes the appointment and hangs up promptly, but not before leaving his phone number with Dubois' assistant. If nobody knows how to reach him, Reddison might drive from Pittsburgh to Cleveland for the meeting, only to find that Dubois is out sick. It happens.

If Dubois' answer is number 2 ("What have you got?"), Reddison answers as follows:

REDDISON: I really can't do it justice by trying to describe this product over the telephone, but when you see the drawings (or prototype) I know you'll be as excited with it as we are. I promise I won't be wasting your time. *(Dubois might press, but Reddison stays firm. He knows NOT to describe his new product idea over the phone. Knowledge is his enemy; curiosity his friend. Dubois relents and the appointment is made.)*

If Dubois' response is number 3 ("You want my partner"), Reddison asks to be switched.

BALDWIN: Hello, Mr. Greenbottom's office.

REDDISON: Hi. My name is Tom Reddison. We create new products for companies. We recently developed something for Global that I spoke to Max about and he wanted me to discuss the idea with Mr. Greenbottom as well—so if you could please put me through, I'd appreciate it. *(Reddison uses the same warm, friendly voice as he did with Dubois' assistant, and, of course, with Max's name mentioned, Baldwin puts the call through without comment. Reddison has a similar conversation with Greenbottom as he had with Dubois and the appointment is made.)*

Except for any waiting time, this conversation will only have taken a few minutes, and almost certainly you'll have your appointment. Never describe your idea over the telephone—it takes the curiosity out of your visit, and you run the risk that Dubois will lose interest, sight unseen. "Can you just give me a hint?" he might say, to which you reply with a warm chuckle and a repeat of your assurance that he's going to be pleasantly surprised when he sees what your team came up with. I've searched my memory, and cannot recall, except for one instance, ever being denied an appointment when I had the right party on the telephone. Every company owner or principal executive wants to know about a product that might be meaningful to the company. These people didn't get where they are by turning their backs on new ideas; they just want assurance that they're not being asked to waste their time with some wild-eyed, weird inventor who will call them all crooks for even suggesting that they are underwhelmed with the idea or know of a similar product, and who will need to be bodily escorted from the office.

Oh, and don't worry that when you do meet with Dubois he will learn that you're really a cashier at a local Walgreens and not the head of some hotshot product development company. By then he'll have your prototype in his hands and it will have been long forgotten.

I'd like to tell you a little story that doesn't exactly put me in a favorable light, but it illustrates some points worth noting.

Remember I said that I can recall only one instance when I didn't get the appointment after speaking to the guy in charge? This is the instance. In fact, I never even got the guy on the phone. I live in

Philadelphia and there was a little company here that made some products that were sold by Staples, OfficeMax, and the other stationery chains. I developed a product that I thought fit into their product line, and although their competitors were larger, I decided to give them the first shot because they were close to home. Lazy slug that I am, it seemed like a sensible move.

I did what I always do—I called the company, telling the phone operator that I had to send a registered letter to the president and needed his name. The woman readily supplied it, and several days later I called again, asking for George Allen (not his real name). A few clicks and the operator was back, "May I know what this is in reference to?" "Sure," I responded, giving her my story about our company having created an exciting new product that we're sure Mr. Allen would want to see. Again a few clicks and then, "I'm sorry, Mr. Allen has stepped away from his desk. Can you call back later?" This was obviously a stall, but I'm a big boy.

Over the next few weeks I called several times and each time, after some back and forth clicks, was told that Mr. Allen had stepped away from his desk. Either he had the worst case of diarrhea the world has ever seen, or he simply decided to never speak to me.

After all my years in business, I had finally met the company owner who had all the new product he needed and didn't want to know about any more. I was sure such a person had to exist somewhere in the world, and now I finally knew who it was.

I suppose I should have just let it go, but this rudeness really made me sore, so I sent him this e-mail:

> Mr. Allen: I called you several times over the past few weeks, each time being told that you had stepped away from your desk. I'm frankly at a loss to understand why you're ducking me. I know it's not personal since we've never met and so I'm puzzled as to why you would refuse to hear about a new product that we're prepared to offer you that might add considerably to your company's profits. If you look us up, you'll see that we're a well-regarded company and obviously wouldn't call if we didn't have a significant reason for doing so. Fortunately for us, there are lots of other companies making product lines similar to yours, so I'm moving on. And when you see an end-display of some great new product at Staples, I promise not to call to remind you that it could have been yours.

> Harvey Reese

That very afternoon I had a message on my voice mail from a "Ms. Jane Smith" (fictitious), who identified herself as the director of marketing for the company and asked that I call, but I never did. If George Allen himself had called, I would have returned the call, but it was obvious to the end that he simply wouldn't meet with me in person. I never did find out why. And it did not give me any satisfaction to learn that by the following year, the company had gone out of business, though I'm not foolish enough to think that my product would have saved it. I tell this little story to make two points:

1. The story stays in my memory because it is such a rare event.

    Over the years I've set up hundreds of appointments for myself with company presidents or division vice presidents, and except for this one instance, I cannot recall ever being denied the appointment. I don't mean to suggest that every meeting ended with a licensing deal—not by a long shot— but these folks will see you if they think you're a responsible person with something worthwhile to show them. Even when the person turns down my product idea, he invariably will invite me to come back when I have something new. What other business is like this? I can't think of any. So please, don't just send out letters or think if you make a website for your product that you're doing something wonderful. You're not.

2. You must always meet with the decision maker and no one else.

    Even though Jane Smith called twice, leaving messages on my machine, I never bothered to call back. I've met with too many Jane Smiths and Joe Smiths over the years, and I don't do it anymore. Ms. Smith might personally be a lovely person, but she's simply a gatekeeper, authorized to say "no," but not to say "yes." Most of the Jane and Joe Smiths of the world are happy with that arrangement because they know that saying "no" won't get them in trouble, but saying "yes" might. Ms. Smith's boss is the only person in that company who could have signed a licensing agreement, and if he wouldn't see me, I was satisfied to move on. Remember, there are lots more companies looking for fresh, innovative new products than there are folks who are capable of creating them, so don't think of yourself as a supplicant when you call for an appointment: View yourself as doing these companies a favor.

IF YOU INSIST ON USING THE MAIL

I am sure I've not convinced every reader about how ineffective it is to submit an idea by mail or e-mail and I realize that some of you have no other choice. And since I can't state categorically that it's *impossible* to do a deal in this manner, I would like to make a suggestion before leaving the subject altogether. Mainly, don't just send a letter or an e-mail to "whom it may concern." Who would respond to that? Call the company, find out the name of the president (assuming a small- to medium-sized company), and give him a call. Introduce yourself to the president in the same way as the script says to do it, except instead of asking for an appointment, tell him that you're placing information about this brilliant new invention in the mail or as an e-mail with an attachment. At least then your recipient can connect a real person to the letter in his hand and will respond differently than he would to an unsolicited mailing. If you send an e-mail with an attachment to just the company, nobody would dare to open it. I get them all the time and I never open an unexpected attachment when I don't know the source; no prudent person would. If circumstances prevent you from making personal visits, talking to the individual before sending the material is certainly the next best way.

And while we're on the subject, never send original material because the recipient is under no obligation to return it since he didn't request the material in the first place. He may mean well, but stray material like this has a way of getting lost in a busy office. And, if you can afford it, send your information by FedEx.

THE CONCEPT OF THE NONDISCLOSURE AGREEMENT: DO YOU SIGN THEIRS, OR DO THEY SIGN YOURS? AND DOES IT MATTER?

There are nondisclosure agreements and disclosure agreements. The nondisclosure agreement is what you give the company to sign—which it won't. The disclosure agreement is what the company gives you to sign—which you must.

For the sake of our discussions, let's assume the product you've invented is an attachment for an automatic lathe. Manufacturers of lathes don't get that many calls from inventors with brilliant new products for them, and so your call for an appointment will go pretty much like our script and you'll be invited to come right over. They might even sign your nondisclosure agreement in order to hear your idea.

On the other hand, if you've created something like a new toy, a new game, or a new kitchen gadget, you will have, unfortunately, joined an army of folks who have also invented those types of products, and the high-profile manufacturers who make them have inventors knocking on their doors all the time. Yes, it's true that these companies go through products quickly, and yes, it's true that they're always on the hunt for something that's excitingly novel and new; however, since these companies have their own design departments hard at work creating a wide range of fresh, new products, they don't want to expose themselves to lawsuits every time an inventor shows them something that they might already be working on themselves. They don't care if you've invented the world's best potato peeler; they won't sign your nondisclosure agreement. And further, they won't look at your brilliant peeler until you sign their own document. That's just the way it is.

**Reading the company's disclosure agreement is
liable to scare the pants off you.**

You wouldn't believe how many e-mails I get from inventors complaining that such and such a company stole their idea and what can they do about it? What usually transpired is that the inventor sent an unsolicited letter to the company and never heard back.

Whether the letter was ever actually read by anyone above the level of mailroom clerk is never known. And then some time later, having seen a similar product by this company in the store, the inventor is convinced that he was ripped off. Companies are aware of this sort of problem, and thus the concept of the disclosure agreement was born.

If you ask any of these companies to sign your nondisclosure agreement before showing them your idea, I think I can safely assure you that they will rarely do it. This refusal is not because they want to steal your idea. Since they're exposed to fresh new product ideas all the time—from both external and internal sources—the chances are better than good that whatever you're planning to show them is something they already know about or are already working on, and so signing your agreement can only lead to problems. The automatic lathe manufacturer, as I say, might sign such an agreement because he has little exposure, but not magnet companies like Rubbermaid or Milton Bradley, where seemingly every customer has a product idea for them. However, as I say, you will be required to sign their own carefully worded legal agreement before they'll at least take a look at your own product idea. It's their game and so you have to agree to play by their rules.

If you've never seen one of these agreements, your first reading is liable to scare the heck out of you. Even if your product idea has six patents, your hands might tremble when you put stamps on your package to send your idea to the company.

Read It and Weep: Contents of a Typical Disclosure Agreement

1. The company says to please not send your idea before you've given it all the legal protection you can because that's the only protection you can count on. Otherwise, proceed at your own risk because the company promises nothing (actually, the inventor often doesn't even have that option; many companies will look only at ideas that are patented).

2. The company reminds you that nobody asked you to send your idea and that you're doing it on your own initiative and at your own risk. Nothing has been promised to you as an inducement. Further, the company reminds you, it's quite possible that it is already working on precisely the idea that you're submitting.

3. And then, just to make sure that you get the point, the document you're required to sign sums it all up:

   A. The company doesn't promise to keep your idea confidential.

   B. The company doesn't promise to return any of your material.

   C. The company doesn't promise to pay you anything.

If your product is patented, which is a requirement for submission by many companies, and if you feel you've been wronged, then it's your patent that you need to rely on, which means lawyers and courts. As the disclosure agreement you were compelled to sign makes abundantly clear, the company did not renege on any promises to you because it promised nothing.

The Mead Corporation is an enlightened company, happy to see whatever new product idea you might wish to show them. If you send the idea by mail, unsolicited, it will be returned unread with the following form letter from the company's legal department, which has allowed me to reprint it here:

> Dear _____
>
> Mead is always receptive to new ideas and new designs, as can be seen from the enclosed write-up, "Mead Welcomes New Ideas," which also outlines the conditions under which new ideas and designs will be evaluated. If you agree with the conditions as set forth in the write-up, please sign and return the form as indicated, together with the idea or design that you would like Mead to evaluate, to my attention at the above address. Your design or idea will then be evaluated and, thereafter, we will relay to you the results of the evaluation.
>
> Thank you for considering Mead in this manner. We look forward to hearing from you in the near future.
>
> Very truly yours,

Included with the letter is the following:

MEAD WELCOMES NEW IDEAS

The Mead Corporation welcomes ideas or designs and will evaluate outside submissions of the ideas or designs that relate to our business. Of course we are not interested in ideas or designs that we may already know about or that are in the public domain. We have many projects on which we are now working and many inventions of our own that have not yet been put into operation.

To protect you as well as ourselves, we must follow definite procedure in handling such ideas and designs.

WHAT SUBJECTS ARE ACCEPTABLE

Your idea should encompass a new or improved process, machine product, composition of matter, or design relative to some phase of the Mead business. In general, Mead's interests include paper and related products, paperboard and related products, metals and minerals, interior furnishings, consumer and educational products, pulp and forest products, and information technology.

DESIGN SUBMISSIONS

Frequently, designs and ideas for the use of certain designs are submitted to Mead. These designs are often in the form of drawings, sketches, photographs, or the like. You should note that mere suggestions are treated by the law as abstract ideas and only the specific embodiments or expressions are subject to protection by design patents or copyrights. Therefore, you must keep in mind that in submitting your design to Mead for evaluation you agree that your submission is limited to the particular design(s) submitted and does not encompass whatever marketing or other generic concept might be associated with such design(s). By way of example, if you submit a photograph of a scenic river and suggest its use on notebook covers, your submission is limited to the specific representation appearing in the photograph you submit and would not extend to other natural scenes, whether or not such scenes include scenic rivers.

YOUR PROTECTION

The United States patent system protects inventors against unauthorized use of their inventions, and the United States copyright system affords protection to authors against copying of their work. Therefore, for the protection of both you and Mead, you must understand that, in submitting and thus disclosing an idea or design to us, you rely upon your patent or copyrights, present or future, for your protections against unauthorized use of your idea or design. You should fully protect your idea or design to your own satisfaction before submitting it for our consideration. You should bear in mind that by submitting your idea to Mead under a non-confidential relationship, you may well be jeopardizing or forfeiting patent rights in certain foreign countries in which you have not yet filed patent applications.

HOW TO SUBMIT YOUR IDEA

We prefer that you either apply for or obtain a patent or copyright your design before sending it to us. When this proves impossible, make a written record of your idea or design in duplicate, sign and date both copies, and have one or more persons to whom you have explained the idea or design sign and date them too. One of the copies can then be submitted to us under the conditions outlined herein. Keep the other copy. While such a written record does not, of itself, give patent or copyright protection, it would be of use in proving priority of invention, should the need arise. Further, this provides a record of what you disclose to us.

WHAT HAPPENS AFTER THE MATERIAL IS SUBMITTED

When we receive the completed form and your written idea or design, we will examine the form and subject matter. Any written idea or design which is not attached to a completed and signed form or does not deal with the subject matter previously listed will be returned to you. If your idea or design is properly submitted and the subject matter is within the range of our interest, we will review it and give you our evaluation of it. And here, in conclusion, are the conditions you must agree to before sending your new product concept to the Mead Corporation:

CONDITIONS OF SUBMISSION

1. All submissions or disclosures of ideas and designs are voluntary on the part of the submitter. No confidential relationship is to be established or implied from consideration of the submitted material.

2. With respect to unpatentable or uncopyrightable ideas and designs, Mead will consider them only with the understanding that the use to be made of such ideas and designs and the compensation, if any, to be paid for them are matters resting solely in the discretion of the company.

3. With respect to patentable or copyrightable ideas and designs, including those covered by patent pending, patent applications, and registered or unregistered copyrights, Mead will consider them only with the understanding that the submitter agrees to rely for his protection wholly on such rights as he may have under the patent and copyright laws of the United States. With respect to ideas and designs included in this subsection, Mead may want to negotiate with the submitter about acquiring rights therein.

4. It is understood that idea and design submissions or disclosures are limited to the specific embodiment or expression submitted and do not extent to any marketing concept or other generic concept which may be associated with said specific embodiment or expression.

5. The foregoing conditions may not be modified or waived.

As forbidding and draconian as these documents might sound, the conditions are not unreasonable from the standpoint of the Mead Corporation's point of view, and they are almost the exact conditions of any other large, high-profile company that you might contact. The bright side is that these companies have no intention of stealing your idea, and if they like what you show them, they'll be happy to negotiate with you for its use.

This document is to protect the company from the crazies that walk the earth; since that description doesn't apply to you, I suggest you just sign on the dotted line and get your idea into play. After all, what choice do you have?

If I call a person for an appointment to show him my idea, and if he tells me I have to sign a disclosure agreement in order for us to meet, I'll have him e-mail it over and I immediately fax it back, signed, often while the two of us are still on the telephone. Yes, certainly a person should always read whatever he's being asked to sign, but I have faith in the intent of these documents and I have faith in the idea that some big company doesn't want the reputation of stealing ideas from the people who submit them.

Some attorneys will advise their clients to always have a non-disclosure agreement signed by the company before disclosing the idea. This advice is well meaning, and for some types of companies, like the lathe manufacturer that we've been using as an example, it will work—but seldom will a manufacturer of consumer products dealing with new product ideas all the time sign such a document. It doesn't hurt to ask, but don't be surprised or suspicious at the answer.

Now, with the appointment made, we're ready to move on to my favorite part of the C.R.A.S.H. program: S as in Sell. You're ready to meet with the person who, if you say the magic words, might be ready to pay you a fortune for your new product idea. What are those magic words? Read on.

7

GETTING TO "YES"

Simple and Easy Steps to Successfully Present Your New Invention or Idea

If you want to sell a car and you spend five dollars to wash and polish it and then apply a little extra elbow grease, suddenly you find you can charge an extra four hundred dollars.

—Donald Trump

W. Clement Stone, a businessman and author, once famously remarked that sales are contingent on the attitude of the salesperson, not the attitude of the prospect. We already know the attitude of the prospect, in this instance the prospective licensee. I would characterize it as "hopeful." After all, he wouldn't have agreed to invite you to his office if he wasn't hopeful that you had some brilliant new product or program to sell him. He's ready to buy, and by the time you finish reading this chapter, you'll be ready to sell. It's easy; trust me.

I'm one of the lucky people in the world because I love the work I do. I wear jeans almost every day, I shave about twice a week, and while everyone is rushing to work, I'm enjoying my second cup of coffee. I work at home, at my own pace, and every month the royalty checks arrive in my mailbox.

"Do what you like to do, and the money will follow." I've heard that advice offered countless times over the years, usually by someone older to someone younger. It didn't make sense to me when I was a young man, just as it probably doesn't make much sense to young people today, but I've come to appreciate the wisdom because I'm living proof that it works. Until middle age, everything I did was for the purpose of making money, whether I liked what I was doing or not. Finally, with near-bankruptcy staring me in the face, I decided to change careers. "To heck with it," I thought to myself, "I'm just going to do what I like to do and I'll do it as best as I know how—and whatever happens, happens." And that's what I did, and sure enough, the money did follow.

I like all parts of what I do, but the part that I like the most is when I take my latest product idea or invention under my arm and go out to sell it. It's a special event because I get to put on a jacket and I get to go someplace. And what could be more rewarding than getting someone excited about an invention or an idea for one that resulted from your own creativity? It's the Rolls-Royce of selling. Do it once successfully, and you won't be able to wait until you can do it again. And the money's not bad either.

PITCHING YOUR TV SHOW IDEA

There is no perfect pitch and no perfect formula, but there are certain principles and attitudes that can make one meeting go better than the next. The best meeting, of course, is the one that results in a sale, but a hundred individuals will have a hundred ways of arriving at that positive result. Depending on your budget, you might like to develop what's known as a sizzle reel or sizzle deck to show at your meeting. A sizzle reel is a brief (5 to 10 minutes) but dramatic and persuasive visual summary of your idea that, hopefully, has enough sizzle to it to spark the interest of your audience. Anything that supports your brilliant idea goes on a sizzle reel—animation, music, and special effects. However, since it is to be viewed by professionals, if you don't have the resources to make something impressive, then perhaps it's best to not make it at all. If you do like the idea of a sizzle reel, however, there is a lot of student talent with fresh, original ideas available at any art school. All things being equal, whether you invest in a sizzle reel or not, if you pay heed to the following suggestions, they will hopefully give you an edge.

It is so difficult to get a pitch meeting with someone in the industry who actually has the power to do something with your idea that when you do get one, you want to be sure you do it right. Your meeting will probably be brief—10 to 15 minutes—and so you want to be fully prepared to say what needs to be said during that period. I don't mean that you should have a memorized presentation; unless you're a brilliant actor, everyone will know you're just saying lines and will be turned off by it. But that doesn't mean you can't have preplanned what you'd like to say. Here are some pitch tips that might help create a great meeting; some are unique to this situation, and others are just good nuts and bolts salesmanship principles that have proven effective over the years.

1. If you've had a successful career in a field that has a direct bearing on the idea or the TV industry, this is the time to present it. If your credentials are impressive, people will play closer attention. However, if you have no important connections you certainly shouldn't lie and give yourself an imaginary resume, but you also needn't discuss your background at all. Let the merits of the idea speak for themselves.

2. Practice your pitch and find some friends or relatives who will listen and ask questions. If there are parts that they don't understand, the person you're pitching to probably won't understand either. Redo it until you get it right.

3. While no one wants to hear a memorized presentation, there's nothing wrong with you having referral notes to make sure you cover all the points you'd like to make. Besides, if you try to make a memorized presentation and get stopped by a question or an interruption in the meeting, you'll probably fumble around trying to remember where you left off. How embarrassing!

4. Don't trash other shows that your own show would be competing with. No salesperson directly trashes a competitor because it seems mean-spirited and lacking in sportsmanship. The executive you're pitching to will think less of you if you take this approach. There's nothing wrong with strongly pointing out your own show's superior competitive features, but do it in a way without saying the other show stinks.

5. Don't make rash claims or promises that have no foundation in fact. If you brag about how many millions of viewers the show will have, anyone at the meeting will know that you're simply talking through your hat and wasting their time. Similarly, if you're asked questions for which you have no qualified answer—like, What do you think the cost per episode would be?—if you don't know, just say so. They won't hold that against you, but they will if you try to bluff.

6. Bring several copies of your treatment to the meeting because you don't know how many executives will be attending. And make sure you arrive early. These folks have allotted a time slot for this meeting and will not be happy if they're sitting around, awaiting your arrival.

7. Be flexible and open to ideas and suggestions. If the executive you're pitching is not interested in the idea, she will listen quietly and patiently and then thank you for coming. If the executive is interested, she'll have suggestions to make or questions to ask. Critical participation is a good thing: Why 12 competitors, and not 10? Why four judges, and why not three? Why have the show in this town and not that town? Be open to all ideas and suggestions. If you have reasons why you did it as you did it's fine to state them, but be willing to accept the possibility that the suggestions are improvements, not articles of war.

8. If you're an inventor selling your invention, you have a prototype to put on the manufacturer's desk which, hopefully, will generate its own level of enthusiasm. However, pitching a TV show idea is all about words, and so you want to make them count. Present your idea with enthusiasm; be upbeat, confident, and positive—but don't be a blowhard. Have respect for the

intelligence of your audience and for their ability to separate genuine enthusiasm from phoniness. Any salesperson, whether he's selling steel bridges or coffee mugs, works to make the buyer like him and trust him because the buyer will listen more favorably to what the salesperson has to say. That's just Selling 101.

Also, since first impressions are made quickly and are often everlasting, and since the development if a TV program is a collaborative effort, presenting yourself as affable, charming, and obliging can stand you in good stead. As professional as an executive might be, he or she is still human and will respond more favorably to a warm, friendly smile than to a grouchy frown.

PITCHING YOUR NEW INTERNET BUSINESS IDEA OR SOFTWARE IDEA

If you're pitching your product invention or idea for a TV show, there are special considerations and preparations that are discussed in this chapter. However, if you're pitching an idea for an Internet business or software idea, you don't have to do much more than show up with a bright smile on your face—the material under your arm will do the selling.

The difficult part of licensing your Internet business idea is not in the selling, but in locating the right prospect. Once you find that individual, getting the appointment is easy because you're talking to a motivated buyer. This is someone who wants to buy what you're selling, so it would seem that all you have to do is provide the reason. However, I think you have to do more. It's fine that you found someone who wants to license the idea and run it—and pay you a cut of the proceeds—but are you sure this is the person who can make the business prosper?

If you were looking for investors instead of a licensee, it would be different because it's you, yourself, that the investors would be buying. They would need to be convinced that not only was the business idea sound, but that you possessed the intelligence, abilities, and vision to make it successful. However, in this instance, since you're turning over your unique business asset to someone else to manage, I think the tables are turned. You shouldn't jump at the first cash-rich person who has expressed interest in the business if he seems half asleep in his chair. Not only does the person need to have the necessary amount of money, but you want to be sure he or she has the skills, ambition, and dedication to make the business soar. Your income is dependent on this person's qualifications, so it doesn't hurt to pick and choose. If you have doubts, I suggest you at least pause and give the relationship some thought before simply plunging ahead. If one person is interested in the business, there will be others. I've walked away from deals a few times because something didn't smell right, and I have never regretted it. If you have a great Internet business idea with an asset that gives a person a unique advantage, plenty of folks with money and time on their hands will be interested, so pick the best partner you can find.

If you have a visionary idea for a software program—something that's the answer to an obvious need that's doable and that no one has thought of—and if you whisper this idea to the right company, that company might develop it and pay you a royalty on whatever it sells. Your chances, however, would be improved considerably if you had a prototype to show how the program would work. If you're a genius code writer, and if your software idea is breathtaking in its possibilities, a company will perhaps pay you to develop it based on a prototype. When 19-year-old Mark Zuckerberg (the founder of Facebook) created the concept for a music recommendation program called Synapse, both AOL and Microsoft wanted to pay him almost a million dollars to develop it—but Zuckerberg turned it down because it would have meant dropping out of school. Of course, now he could probably take a million dollars out of the petty cash drawer.

However, while few might have his genius or vision, that doesn't mean that similar success couldn't be achieved at a different level, particularly if you're an established software developer with a proven record.

And, finally, if you went to the same company with a completely developed program that all they have to do is put their name on, then getting a licensing deal would perhaps be a no-brainer. At that point the program would speak for itself, and it wouldn't matter if you wrote it yourself or had it done for you. However, you're going from zero investment to a substantial one, so much depends on your resources, skills, and level of commitment.

Or, if the software idea is at the app level, and if you want to use it to promote your main business, you might do what I did and pay a developer to create it for you. There are lots of freelance developers around. When I was checking costs for my own purposes, I was getting local bids and also bids from developers in the Philippines, Turkey, and Australia. This really is a global village.

PITCHING YOUR NEW PRODUCT INVENTION

I realize that some things are easier said than done, but that doesn't mean they're not worth saying anyway. Not being easy doesn't mean impossible. I urge you to approach each sales call with the confidence that the prospects will love what you're getting ready to show them. The late, famous Dale Carnegie called it the power of positive thinking.

I don't know why it works, but it does. Every professional executes with the anticipation of success. The professional golfer expects to hole the putt, the quarterback expects to complete the pass, and every baseball player comes to bat expecting to get a hit. If these athletes didn't visualize and expect success with every action, they wouldn't be where they are.

It's this kind of attitude that all good salespersons have as well—and they don't even have the satisfaction of selling their own creation. Very few people have the ability to create a commercially viable new product idea, and even fewer of them have the perseverance to bring it to the point of having a meeting with a potential licensee. That's where you find yourself now, and you should carry yourself into the meeting with pride and confidence. Doing so will reflect in your voice and your body language, and most of all it will reflect on the product idea you're presenting. Your accomplishment commands respect, and you'll receive it. Keep in mind that the person on the other side of the desk is not your enemy. That person wants to like you and wants to like the idea you're selling. He wouldn't be sitting across from you if he didn't.

A SALESPERSON'S WORST NIGHTMARE (PART 1)

Some years ago I had an appointment with a company president whom I had never met before. I showed up for my appointment a few minutes early and was kept in a small, windowless reception room for about 40 minutes. At my request, on a couple of occasions the receptionist called to ask about the delay and was told "soon." Finally I was ushered into the great woman's office. I wasn't greeted with an apology or even a hello.

In fact, as I recall, I wasn't even offered a seat. Instead, as I entered, the president looked up from her paperwork to announce that she was very busy and could only give me 10 minutes. I should mention that she knew I had to drive more than two hours to get to her office. What she might not have known is how angry I was to have been kept waiting for almost an hour with not even the courtesy of an apology.

I've been in this business too long to just stand there and have terms dictated to me, so I announced that what I had to show her would take more than 10 minutes and that maybe one day, if the product was still available, I'd come back and we could start over. With that I simply turned and left, but not before noticing the stunned look on her face.

Within two weeks her assistant called me no less than three times to ask if I was ready to reschedule. Each time I told her no, I wasn't. I never did go back, licensing the product instead to one of her competitors. To tell the truth, the product wasn't that big of a deal and she didn't miss much, but she never knew it. In her mind, who knows what a big opportunity she allowed to slip past? It's not a matter of being cocky—if I didn't have someplace else to place the product I probably would have gone back—and maybe we would have become friends. But that's not the point: My point is that you are the king or queen of the hill, not the manufacturer. There are lots of manufacturers, but not many folks like us who can bring them profitable, original, new product ideas, one after another. If I can persuade you to think of yourself that way, then making the sales call is child's play.

A SALESPERSON'S WORST NIGHTMARE (PART 2)

As a very young man I had a job as a salesperson on the road. On my very first day, on my very first call, I had an experience that will stay with me forever. I was calling on a supermarket buyer, waiting in the lobby to be called along with a roomful of other sales representatives also waiting to see one buyer or another. It was first come, first called. As the receptionist called one salesperson after another, my nervousness kept increasing—first call ever—what would it be like?

Finally it was my turn, and I was directed to my buyer's office, which, as I later discovered, was a typical grocery buyer's office: small, airless, piled high with papers and samples, furnished with scarred, nicked, old wooden furniture. I felt like I was visiting a cheap detective to ask him to take my case. The buyer himself just sat there silently, looking me over with hooded eyes—no smile, no greeting. I said hello; he nodded. Once I was settled in my chair, nervous about how to proceed, he reached over, cranked an egg timer that was placed in front of me, and said, "Okay, kid, you've got three minutes."

To my credit, I didn't pass out. The ticking of the egg timer was like Big Ben in my ears, each tick tock bringing me closer to my doom. Flustered, embarrassed, and rattled, I broke all records racing though my presentation, probably not taking more than two minutes, plunked down my catalog sheets, mumbled my thanks, and left. I was humiliated.

I'd like to tell you that he actually placed an order and that we ultimately became good friends, but he didn't and we didn't. What I got out of the experience, however, was much more valuable. What I got was the resolve to never again allow myself to be treated this way by a buyer—and it never did happen again. That is, not until 30 years later when the president I just talked about gave me 10 minutes for my presentation. From three minutes to 10 minutes is not much progress when you allow for inflation.

In between these two episodes I've had more pleasant and productive meetings than I could ever count or remember. However, these two events stand out because, thankfully, they're so rare. When you meet with your own prospect I can almost guarantee that you'll be treated with hospitality and consideration. The person you're meeting with will assuredly greet you in an anticipatory mood, hoping you have something wonderful to present. Executives love to see interesting new products; it's the lifeblood of their business. Other salespeople selling other things would be thrilled to have their prospects greet them in this frame of mind.

ESTABLISHING YOUR CREDENTIALS

As discussed, when pitching an idea for a TV show, it's a time-pressure meeting, usually only about 10 minutes, and so the creator is under the gun to say what he or she has to say as crisply, efficiently, and persuasively as possible without missing a beat. That's why these folks rehearse ahead of time. However, if you're meeting with a manufacturing executive to show your new product invention, they will usually allow the meeting to go on for as long as it seems productive. Nevertheless, if you start repeating yourself or start wandering, they will rise from their chair, shake your hand, and thank you for coming in. That doesn't mean that you have to rehearse your pitch like the TV show creator does, but it does mean that you have to keep on target.

First, if you have any credentials relevant to the invention, this is the time to establish them. If you're a veterinarian with a new pet product idea, that should be the first thing you mention. However, if your professional experience is as an accountant with an idea for a new pet product, I think it's best to skip that part. The whole point of establishing credentials is to persuade the prospect to take you seriously. Having a professional association with the product is one way to do it, but not the only way. How you dress and what you say can make an indelible mark.

Allowing for obvious differences, male and female executives dress the same way in similar circumstances. A female marketing executive for a Fortune 500 company projects the same sartorial image as her male counterpart. If you can dress similarly, you are presenting yourself as belonging to the environment, ready to be accepted into the club.

If you're calling on IBM, you'll probably wear a suit and tie or female equivalent. And if your idea is for Facebook, jeans and a T-shirt is probably the right attire since we know that's virtually a uniform at that company. If you were to switch—showing up at IBM corporate headquarters in jeans and a T-shirt or showing up at Facebook in a three-piece suit—you'd probably not be doing your cause much good. It's easy to dress like you fit in, and it's worth making the effort.

If you were applying for a job with a company, the Human Resources Director, talking to a fellow employee who happened to pass you in the lobby, is apt to ask what you look like. She's not asking if you're handsome or pretty, she's asking if you look like you'll fit in. If you're a guy, don't wear your earrings, and if you're a woman, leave the tight skirt and low blouse at home. All of this matters more than you might think.

Your speech patterns are also carefully noticed because they act as billboards for your attitude. For instance, using excessive slang or teenage idioms sounds silly coming from an adult, and it tends to trivialize you (and your idea). Also, if your prospect is much older than you, you don't want your language to suggest that the old geezer is out of step with the modern way of doing things that your product represents. Similarly, if the prospect is much younger, you're not going to bore the little pipsqueak by talking about how great the old ways of doing things were. And, naturally, politics, race, and religion are off the table. And surely I don't have to remind you to lose the chewing gum.

I know I'm stating the obvious, so just think of these as gentle reminders. When you realize the value of first impressions and how quickly they're subconsciously formed, you can turn that to your advantage by really concentrating on the first few minutes of your meeting. Curmudgeon that you may be, if you can make a conscious effort to present yourself right off the bat as serious, honest, capable, and friendly, in those first few minutes you will have set the tone for the meeting. If you look like and present yourself as someone it would be nice to do business with, then it's more likely to happen. On the other hand, if you walk in looking like trouble, things are not likely to go your way.

SAY HELLO TO THE NEW PRODUCTS DIRECTOR

I know I encouraged you to do a little harmless fibbing to get the appointment, but now that you're actually in the meeting, it's the truth that will set you free. If you puff, exaggerate, or downright lie, it will invariably be found out and not only will you be embarrassed and perhaps made to look foolish, but it might make your prospective licensee wary of entering into the relationship. Let's look at this scenario. You're sitting with Stu Dubois, the company president. He picks up the phone and says, "Frank, do you have a few minutes? I've got a guy in my office with a new product idea that I think you should take a look at." Frank, it turns out, is the company's research and development director and, you must assume, he commands Stu's respect. If you're automatically suspicious that Frank could be a deal-breaker, your instincts are probably correct. This guy's your enemy, a sufferer of the N.I.H. malady, and must be handled gently. It's his department's responsibility to generate the new products for the company; they shouldn't come from some dumb outsider. The trick is to make him look good without making you look bad. Here's a snippet of a conversation that you must avoid.

> STU: So what do you think we can get for this thing?
>
> YOU: I think ten dollars seems about right because, while Consolidated's costs a few dollars less, our model has all these great extra features.
>
> FRANK: So what do you think it'll cost to make? *(Frank is setting his trap, but you're so anxious to please that you plow right ahead.)*
>
> YOU: I've looked at that very closely. I'm confident that it shouldn't cost more than about three dollars, depending on whether you go with plastic or wood.

A smile creeps onto Frank's face because he can see that you didn't do your homework and don't know what you're talking about. Everyone knows that products in the camping business (the business this company is in) need at least a five-time multiplier from cost to retail in order to make a profit. So, if the cost is about $3, as you maintain, then the retail would have to be about $15, but you just said that the idea price should be about $10. So now what? What's wrong: Your estimate of the cost or the estimate of the best selling price—or don't you really know?

The question of cost versus retail comes up at every licensing meeting if there's genuine interest in what you're offering. All products have a perceived value—what a customer can be expected to pay—and so the trick is to be able to produce the product profitably at a level that meets the target retail price. So if we rewind that conversation, it should go like this:

> STU: So what do you think we can get for this thing?
>
> YOU: Gosh, you and Frank know pricing strategy a lot better than I do, but it's certainly worth more than the set that Consolidated is selling. Frank here, I'm sure, can give you a more reliable answer than I can.
>
> FRANK: So what do you think it'll cost?
>
> YOU: Well, the cost I came up with is about three dollars, but I'm sure you have better contacts and a better handle on production

costs than I do. I have no doubt that you can produce it than a lower figure than my estimate. What's your best guess?

Stu and Frank really don't need you to tell them about costs and pricing since they do that every day. This kind of conversation is really just to give Stu a few moments to mull the idea over in his mind. Your job is to avoid acting like an expert in areas where you're not, and at the same time enlisting Frank as your ally. Do that and the rest is easy.

Five Simple Presentation Tips

1. If you have presentation material to offer about the market or the product, don't read it. There's little that can turn a customer off faster than a salesperson sitting in front of him reading from his presentation. The customer's concentration fades and he starts to enjoy watching the birds in the beautiful tree growing outside his office window.

2. If you do have a prepared presentation, don't hand out copies until you've finished making your oral presentation. If you do, the people at the meeting will skim ahead and know what you're about to say before you say it.

3. Move along at a brisk, business-like pace. As already said, one thing that all businesspeople hate is to have their time wasted. If your focus wanders and roams, and you start talking about how much your Aunt Jenny, who's twice divorced and now living with her new boyfriend in Wichita, loves this idea—and how when she mentioned it to your Uncle Ned, her first husband, the one who used to be in the merchant marine, how excited he got and how he told everyone down at the Elks club and how now everybody wants one—you will find that your audience has left and the security guard has entered the room to escort you from the building.

4. Keep your prototype under wraps, and introduce it only at the proper time—and when you do, place it in the customer's hands. It's his product now, not yours.

5. Be conscious of how the meeting is progressing and when you sense it's time to close the deal—*close it!* You'd be amazed at how many salespeople can do everything except ask for the order—and how simply asking for it can make all the difference. Lots of guys can ask a woman to marry him and spend her life with him but can't get up the nerve to ask for an order for a gross of widgets. Amazing.

Rule #1: Never read your presentation.

"But how will I know when it's time to close the deal?" you might ask. What a coincidence! That's just what we're getting to.

The holy grail of good salesmanship can be summed up in one simple sentence: *Think from the customer's point of view and tailor your presentation accordingly.* You can read a dozen books about sales tactics, but they all boil down to that simple truth. As someone famously observed, guys don't want quarter-inch drill bits, they want quarter-inch holes. If you have a better way of making those holes, they'll listen. If you can understand what benefits your customer is really looking for in licensing your product, and if you can show him how licensing will help him achieve that goal, then you can write your own book on salesmanship.

Yes, of course Stu wants to make money by licensing your product—that goes without saying—but there are other things that might make it special. For instance, instead of just telling Stu how many of these products he can sell, suppose you said things like this:

1. Yes, Stu, because there's a real need for this product, you should be able to get quick, national distribution, including in outlets where you're not now selling. This product can provide the entree.

2. Because this product will so obviously sell by itself, all you have to do is put it in a great package. The money you might have spent on advertising can go right into profits.

3. Because this product is so superior to the one that Ajax is selling, (Stu's principal competitor) your salespeople can probably easily get their customers to switch. Kelly over at Ajax will be so mad he'll spit.

Increasing distribution and sticking it to Ajax are far more important to Stu than simply reminding him of the profit he can make from your product. This is called benefit selling, and it's what every good salesperson practices. And what every *really* good salesperson knows is when to ask for the order and isn't embarrassed about doing so.

You Know It's Time to Close the Deal . . .

1. when the conversation moves beyond the merits of the invention or product idea itself and onto more practical matters such as production costs, packaging, and marketing. In the manufacturer's mind the product is his, and so production and marketing are the next steps in the process of bringing it to market. That's why I urge you, assuming it's a consumer product, to present the prototype in a good-looking, selling package.

2. when the person you're meeting with calls another person into the meeting and that person shows enthusiasm for the idea. The person you're working with has made up his mind to buy, but he's looking for confirmation. If the person called in is an assistant that you've met before and were pleasant with, that's a plus. If it's someone you don't know—well, you know your mission. Treat this person with respect and dignity and get him or her on your side.

3. when the prospective licensee keeps playing with your prototype with a proprietary air—which is more possible if the prototype is attractive, well made, and easily shows that it does the promised job.

When I was a salesperson on the road, if I felt that my customer was ready to buy after finishing my presentation, I would simply take out my order form and, with pencil poised, give ordering suggestions. "It comes in three colors: red, blue, and orange. Orange is the slowest seller and blue is the best seller. I suggest each dozen be packed two orange, four red, and six blue." And he'd probably say something like, "Do I really need the orange?" And after that it's just details.

Now, when selling a product license, I do the same thing. If I'm dealing with someone new, and I believe he likes the product, I'll take out my licensing agreement (like every good salesperson, I always have one in my briefcase) and will say something like, "This standard licensing agreement is very simple, and I'm sure there's nothing in here that will bother you. Shall we go over it?" Or, often, even before I do that, the customer will simply say, "So what's the deal?" I'll respond with, "Five percent royalty, $10,000 advance against future earnings." That's all he wants to hear; the rest are details that he knows and I know will be worked out to our satisfaction. The fact that I already have an agreement in my bag says it's standard, and so there's nothing in it for him to fear.

Stu might like the product, but he's having a hard time saying yes (he never has a hard time saying no). He's pleading with you, in his own way, to give him a little nudge. "Well, I do like the product," he might say, "but what with the economy the way it is, and money's tight . . ." And you'll say, "I understand, I don't mind. But to be honest, Stu, when I made this appointment with you I also made one with United and Mogul, but I came here first because you're the company I want to deal with so I'm in a bit of a box. I don't mind cancelling my other appointments, but I don't want to do that and later find out I shouldn't have." The thought that one of his two worst enemies, George (that no-good thief) at United or Herb (that lousy liar) at Mogul might have the product is usually enough to persuade Stu to move ahead.

A CUSTOMER'S TWO CENTS WORTH

So far, everything discussed has been from our point of view, the seller's, and so I thought it would be interesting to see what a buyer had to say on the subject. Tory Bers, a friend of mine, is the person in charge of product development for a toy company. Part of her job is to interview inventors with ideas to present, so I asked her for a few pointers. Here are some of the things she mentioned.

- *Make Sure Your Presentation Doesn't Look Shopworn.* That's an excellent suggestion that I should have made myself. If your presentation material looks crinkled and worn, it's obvious that it has been shopped around quite a bit and that this prospective licensee is just one of a list that you're going through—no following no. That's certainly not the impression you want to make. If you're a guy proposing to a woman, you're not going to say, "Shirley, I've been turned down three times already by others, and so I hope you'll agree to say yes." Even if it's true, Shirley doesn't need to know. You have to make Shirley believe that she's the one and only. Similarly, if your presentation material suggests the same thing, that others have rejected you time and time again, the guy you're sitting in front of now is not going to be inclined to say yes. To you, he's Shirley, and crisp, fresh presentation material will make him feel he's the only one.

- *Don't Oversell.* Make your presentation once. Do it thoroughly and with enthusiasm, but don't get too aggressive. Be truthful and straightforward. You're dealing with seasoned, professional businesspeople, so if you push too hard, you're going to make enemies instead of friends. When in doubt, pause to listen. Many times that will get you further than just talking and talking.

- *Be Flexible, Easygoing, and Helpful.* If you come across as rigid, unpleasant, and bullheaded, the prospect might fear that there will be problems dealing with you down the road. If the customer is on the fence about your product, your attitude might be the deciding factor. When the caveman Zoggo, the world's first professional salesperson, first started in his career, he used to hit his prospects on the head with a rock to get their attention. Zoggo sold stone wheels, and sales in his territory were terrible. Finally, one day, instead of bonking his prospect, he smiled and asked about the kids. His prospect had never seen a smile before but knew he liked it, and it generated warm feelings toward Zoggo. Since then, sales for Zoggo's stone wheels soared, and he was soon able to move his family into a charming three-chamber cave where they lived happily ever after. And since that time, over the years, the lore has been passed on from salesperson to salesperson, "You'll get more with a smile than with a whack on the head."

- *Come to the Meeting Properly Dressed.* We already discussed this, so I'm glad Tory Bers mentioned it. Businesspeople are like everyone else; they prefer dealing with those who seem to be most like them, sharing the same values. Dress in the same manner as your prospect, and you'll go a long way in making that impression.

After all the work you did in creating and preparing your new product, invention, software, business, or TV game show idea, and after preparing and sweating through your presentation, it's a once-in-a-lifetime thrill when the person you're pitching stands up, extends his hand and say, *"Let's do the deal!"* Deal? What deal? Perhaps your thinking didn't take you that far, but it will after you read the next chapter. It's harvest time, and the right contract will earn you all the fruits of your labor to which you're entitled.

8

REAPING THE HARVEST

Sometimes I wake up at night and ask, "Where have I gone wrong?" Then a voice says to me, "This is going to take more than one night."

—Charlie Brown

When the prospect says, "Yes, let's do the deal!" that can mean different things, depending on what you're selling. If a TV production company says, "Yes, let's do the deal!" after hearing your idea for a new reality show, that's not the same thing as a kitchen gadget company saying it after seeing your idea for a new potato peeler. It's like comparing the pig's contribution to your breakfast to the hen's. Nevertheless, a deal is still a deal, and a contract is still a contract, so much of it is the same. But there are some important differences that are worth noting.

THE DEAL FOR YOUR TV GAME SHOW OR REALITY SHOW

If you're licensing your potato peeler, then the deal really is the deal. Once the kitchen gadget company says "yes," you both sign the contract, you receive your advance money, and you go about your business. From then on it's up to the kitchen gadget company to make the molds, produce, and sell the peeler. All you have to do is cash the checks that come every month. However, when the TV production company says, "Yes!" what they're saying is "Yes—maybe." The only deal that they're making with you at the moment is buying your permission to show the idea to a couple of appropriate networks. If the networks say "No deal," then that's what it is—no deal. Most TV networks won't deal with you directly because, even if you have a great idea, you don't have the contacts, facilities, or experience to develop and produce the show, so why bother? They will deal with an agent, so if you have an agent to represent you that's all to the good; but even if the network responds positively to the idea, the agent still has to connect you with the production company, and the deal, whatever it is, is still temporary unless or until a contract is actually signed with the network.

Here's how it usually works: Either directly or through an agent, you will have met with the production company and, for our purposes, we're assuming they love your idea. The production company will be ready to sign an option and what's referred to as a deal memo with you, and at this point it's probably advisable to have an entertainment lawyer at your side. The option part of the agreement is easy—for a nominal sum, say a few thousand dollars, the production company will option the idea for a few weeks or months to give the executives time to develop and present the idea to the appropriate networks. The deal memo is the agreement part that the two of you settled on as your reward if the network likes the idea and the production company exercises its option to acquire the rights from you. In other words, the deal is made on paper even if it never happens. The only money the production company is obligated to pay you is the few thousand dollars for the option. Everything else, as we say, is on the come. That's where your lawyer comes in.

Since I assume you're not a famous director or producer with lots of contacts and credits, the production company does not view you as someone who can contribute in any way to the program's success, so the company's intent will be to simply say thanks, pay you off, and tell you to go away. Someone from the company might even drive you to the airport. However, you don't want to be kissed off so easily, and that's how your entertainment lawyer earns his fee.

How big the purchase price might be depends on what can be negotiated; there is no magic number. Also, your attorney will work hard to get you to receive a small (really small) percentage of the fees paid to the production company by the network. Also, he might be able to gain the rights to have your name on the screen as "Created by" or "Consulting Producer" or something that will give you bragging rights back home. There is no one-size-fits-all agreement on these matters—you get what you can negotiate for. There are lots of kinds of deals where you don't need an attorney, but for this kind of deal you do. Since you're swimming with sharks, you might as well have one of your own.

THE DEAL FOR YOUR SOFTWARE PROGRAM

Your target for a licensing partner would be a software publisher who's selling a software program or programs to the same customer that your own software is intended for—but one that is not in competition with the publisher's own programs. It is the publisher's responsibility to produce and package the program, set the retail price, and develop a marketing plan to gain maximum distribution (usually simply called "best efforts"). The use of the program is usually awarded on an exclusive basis.

Your job as the developer is to deliver the program in a timely manner that has been both alpha and beta tested and to attest to the fact that you are the developer and owner. You would also be obligated to fix any program problems that might arise and to educate the publisher's technical support team. You might also be responsible for creating upgrades as warranted, and a typical agreement will prohibit you from developing any competitive programs for others.

Payment to you, the developer, would be a nonrefundable cash advance and royalties. The royalty is usually between 10 and 15 percent and is normally based on net receipts (not gross). Net receipts is usually defined as gross receipts, the sum received from the publisher's customer, minus any applicable taxes, shipping costs, cash discounts, and customer returns. Sometimes the royalty percentage can be lower at the outset and scaled upward after the publisher has sold an agreed-upon number of programs, presumably enough to recoup their initial investment. The publisher might be obligated to guarantee you a minimum payment to keep the agreement intact.

There are, of course, lots of standard clauses common in most distribution contracts, such as the right to examine books, arbitration, rights under cancellation, warranties, indemnifications, and so on, but those are the main points.

If the level of your relationship to the prospective licensee is confined to giving him simply the software idea in exchange for royalties, then the contract between you and the publisher would be similar. But since the publisher is doing all the work and making all of the financial investment, the advance would be much less, as would the royalty percentage paid, perhaps in the neighborhood of 2 percent.

If you've presented a demo prototype and are asking the publisher for money to complete the program, that, too, would basically be the same agreement and the money advanced would be applied against future earned royalties. A principal difference is that in this case, unlike in an agreement for the potato peeler invention, the software prototype advance is refundable. If you fail to deliver the completed software program under the terms of the agreement, you would be legally obligated to return the advance and the publisher would, of course, have the right to call off the deal.

If you're turning over a fully developed software program, then the agreement is straightforward and would essentially be the same as any other licensing agreement, such as the one I use, which will be reviewed and dissected in this chapter.

THE DEAL FOR YOUR PRODUCT INVENTION

Since this book is about product licensing, I'm assuming that for good reason you've thought about marketing the product yourself and have decided against it. I'm also assuming that you have developed your product idea or invention, have pursued the licensing route, and now find yourself in the prospect's office. You've just completed a brilliant presentation, and the prospect leaps to his feet, grabs your hand to shake, and exclaims, "Fabulous! Let's make a deal!" So now what?

There are two things I'd like you not to say: One is bad; the other is worse (much worse). The bad thing to say is that you'll have your attorney draw up a licensing deal to submit to him. If the executive wants to do the deal—*do it now, at this instant!* The attorney can later add the legalese, but if you wait for him to draw up the agreement, anything can happen in the interim and the prospect's enthusiasm for the product might fade or even disappear as your natural enemies in the company take pot shots at it. Maybe your guy gets fired, or maybe the company gets bought, or maybe a competitor comes out with something similar. Anything can happen while you're sitting around waiting for your lawyer to get around to making up a contract for you.

And even worse than saying your attorney will draw up the agreement is to suggest that the prospect's own attorney draw it up. Believe me, you don't what to do that. The prospect is the attorney's client, so naturally the agreement he or she draws up will be the licensing agreement from hell. The terms will be so draconian that you'll seemingly wind up paying the prospect just for taking the invention off your hands. I repeat: Don't do that.

Licensing agreements needn't be complicated to give you what you're entitled to—and to give the licensee everything he's entitled to as well—so the two of you can negotiate an agreement in short order with no lawyers in sight. It's a business agreement that the two of you can put together without breaking a sweat. You'll give a little and the prospective licensee will give a little, and before you know it, the deal will be done. The trick, of course, is for him to give a little more than you do. I'm going to show you how to make that happen.

Rule #4: Never let the licensee's attorney draw up the licensing agreement.

THE GENTLE ART OF NEGOTIATING

I remember once reading a feature article in the *New York Times* written by a reporter who visited a dozen individually owned stores on upper Broadway in Manhattan to see if she could negotiate better deals for herself. Amazingly, she was successful 10 of the 12 times.

> "I love these shoes, but they're a little more than I can afford to spend. If you give me 10 percent off, I'll take them right now."

> "This dress is perfect, but it needs that scarf to go with it. I can't afford to pay for both—so if you could throw in the scarf for free, I'm ready to write the check."

I made up that dialogue, but I'm sure it resembles what transpired. Give a little; get a little. The reporter gets the garments; the shopkeeper gets the sale. It's negotiation; you do this, and I'll do that. It doesn't have to mean shouting, yelling, or grinding someone into the dust. In its best form, it's simply coming to a meeting of the minds. The reporter didn't ask for too much, and the shopkeeper made a profit that might have otherwise been lost. Both are happy with the deal. Negotiating is a time-honored craft, and the techniques that work have been identified and refined over the years. Here are the important ones.

1. *Know what you want before you start.* Before you even show up for your appointment, you should have a clear idea what you

want out of the deal. Each of your requests should be reasonable, well thought out, and defensible. After reading this chapter you'll have a good idea of what you have a right to demand, and what you have to be prepared to negotiate. Knowledge will give you confidence, so you won't have to pause or seem hesitant as you progress from point to point in the agreement. If you do, it can seem to be a sign of uncertainty and the prospect might try to take advantage. It's like that old saying about the other guy offering to meet you halfway while he's already standing on the dividing line. It's not difficult to prevent that from happening. If you know the steps, the dance can be fun.

2. *Don't be greedy*. On Wall Street they say that sometimes the bears win and sometimes the bulls win, but the pigs always get slaughtered. Don't be piggish or you might find you're the only person still in the room. If you ask a dozen patent attorneys why a licensing negotiation went sour, the answer will almost always be because of the unreasonable demands from the inventor. To be fair, if I asked a dozen inventors they'd probably say it's because of the ineptitude or posturing of their attorney. But regardless of who's at fault, the probable reason for the breakdown is that more was asked of the licensee than the licensee could accept. While, yes, you are entitled to certain conditions, you have to understand the other side's legitimate needs as well. If you listen intelligently, you can probably accommodate those needs without compromising your own. If you or your attorney continues to make arbitrary demands that the other side can't accept, there will be no deal. Ask for the moon and you'll get the gate. The sample contract later in this chapter offers a clear, sensible balance between the two sides and can guide you to a satisfactory conclusion where both you and your licensee can be satisfied and still be friends. This business is not about one side issuing surrender terms to the other.

3. *Don't get personal*. You must develop a proper perspective about the negotiating process. Whatever transpires, it's not life or death; it's just business. Whatever the outcome, you'll still have your health, you won't go to jail, and no one is holding your first-born child for ransom. Therefore, it's never excusable to raise your voice or to be impolite. Amateurs may do that, but professionals never yell and never curse. If you push, the other side will shove, and soon you'll have a brawl on your hands. What good is that? The purpose of negotiation is to resolve conflict, not create it. As previously observed, people so obviously

respond better to kindness that you have to wonder about those who negotiate with a mean-spirited attitude.

4. *Don't be a patsy.* On the other side of the coin of being too belligerent is being too obliging. Yes, you want to make the deal, but you can't just agree to every demand; and when you do have to say yes, at least try to get something in return. "Okay, if I agree to point B, will you see it my way in Clause 3?" Fair's fair. "Okay, I'll do this if you do that." Sometimes you'll get your way and sometimes not, but at least the other side will see that you know what you're doing and you're not just rolling over.

5. *The fear thing.* The late John F. Kennedy famously said that we should never fear to negotiate, but we should never negotiate out of fear. You have a big advantage over the person you're bargaining with. If he wants your invention, then you can probably find other companies who will also want it. But you're the only one who owns the invention; there are no others. That means that you can walk away from the deal with little damage and go elsewhere, but the other guy can't. You're not going to be so crass as to throw it in his face, but if he understands from the way you present yourself that you'll walk away if your legitimate minimum demands aren't met, that's a powerful weapon. Yes, certainly work to make the deal, but if you have the sense that the other guy isn't dealing from the top of the deck, this is the time to do something about it. I've walked away from deals that didn't smell right to me a few times in my long career, and I never regretted doing so. However, there are some deals that I did make that I later wished I hadn't.

6. *Win by listening.* You can properly assume that the prospective licensee is sitting there negotiating with you not because he has nothing else to do but because he thinks your product invention can make money for his company. He *wants* to do business with you; he *wants* to make the deal. Your job is to make it easy for him by listening closely to what he feels the contract should include and, unless the demands are ridiculous (which would rarely be the case), to figure out a way to accommodate him, or to at least offer a face-saving alternative. The more carefully you listen, the easier that is.

7. *Don't forget about tomorrow.* Now that you're on the verge of licensing your new invention or product idea to this company, there's a good chance you'll be back with another one. The company is now familiar to you; you know the kind of products

they're looking for, and so it's only natural that your creative talents would be steered in that direction. I can remember no company that I licensed one product to that I didn't come back to license the next, and the next after that. If you've maintained yourself in a pleasant and accommodating manner during this negotiation, showing that you're not an unreasonable or bull-headed person to work with, the company president will have a smile on his face the next time you walk into her office with a prototype under your arm.

ONE MORE HINT

These negotiations aren't difficult to begin with, but they're a lot easier if you already have printed copies of your contract in your briefcase to place on the table at the proper time and that's what you negotiate from. By doing that you are like the guy I mentioned—the one standing on the dividing line offering to meet the other party halfway. The fact that it's a preprinted document suggests that you do these deals all the time and this is the standard agreement used by everyone. Do this and you'll save yourself lots of grief. My own agreement, which I welcome you to use, was written by me, not a lawyer (although it was vetted by one), and so it reads like a straightforward business deal without a lot of legalese and hidden little bits of fine print that no one can read or understand. As you'll see, it's obviously fair and licensees seldom see a need to make changes. But, deceptively simply though it may be, it does give you all the rights you're entitled to.

The Harvey Reese Standard Invention Licensing Agreement

Harvey Reese Associates, located at _____
(hereinafter referred to as **LICENSOR**) has given _____
_____ located at _____
_____ (hereinafter referred to as **LICENSEE**)

the exclusive production and marketing rights to his new product concept or invention as herein described and as per patents, patent applications, drawings and/or prototype samples previously submitted. In exchange, LICENSEE agrees to pay LICENSOR an advance and royalties in the amount and under the terms outlined in this Agreement.

PRODUCT DESCRIPTION:

A. ROYALTY PAYMENTS. A _____% (_____percent) royalty based on net selling price will be paid by LICENSEE to LICENSOR on all sales of subject product or invention and all subsequent variations thereof by LICENSEE, its subsidiaries and/or associate companies. The term "net selling price" shall mean the price LICENSEE receives from its customers, less any discounts for volume, cooperative promotion funds, defects, freight or credit returns. Royalty payments shall be paid monthly, by the 30th day of the month following shipment to LICENSEE'S customers, and LICENSOR shall have the right, upon 10 days notice, to examine LICENSEE'S books and records as they pertain thereto. Further, LICENSEE agrees to reimburse LICENSOR for any legal costs he may incur in collecting overdue royalty payments; assuming the suit is successful. If not successful, legal costs are paid by the LICENSOR.

2. TERRITORY. LICENSEE shall have the right to market this product throughout the United States, its possessions and territories, Canada, and Mexico. It may do so through any legal distribution channel it desires and in any manner it sees fit without prior approval from LICENSOR. However, LICENSEE agrees it will not knowingly sell to parties who intend to resell the product(s) outside of the licensed territory.

3. ADVANCE PAYMENT. Upon execution of this agreement LICENSEE will make a nonrefundable payment to LICENSOR in the amount of $_____, which shall be construed as an advance against future earned royalties.

4. COPY, PATENT, AND TRADEMARK NOTICES. LICENSEE agrees that on the product, the packaging, and collateral material there shall be printed notices of any patents issued or pending and any applicable copyright and/or trademark notices to showing the LICENSOR as the owner of said patents, trademarks, and copyrights under exclusive license to LICENSEE. In the event that there has been no previous registration or patent application for the licensed product(s), LICENSEE may, at LICENSEE'S discretion and expense, make such application or registration in the name of the LICENSOR. However, LICENSEE agrees that at the termination or expiration of this Agreement, LICENSEE will be deemed to have assigned, transferred, and conveyed to LICENSOR all trade rights, equities, titles, or other rights in and of the licensed property that may have been attained by the LICENSEE. Any

such transfer shall be without consideration other than as specified in this Agreement.

5. TERMS AND WARRANTS. This Agreement shall be deemed to be in force for so long as LICENSEE continues to sell the original product or subsequent extensions or variations thereof. However, it is acknowledged that LICENSEE has made no warrants to LICENSOR in regard to minimum sales and/or royalty payments guarantees. Further, LICENSOR agrees that, for the life of the Agreement, he or she will not create and/or provide directly competitive products to another manufacturer or distributor without giving the right of first refusal to LICENSEE.

6. PRODUCT DESIGNS. LICENSOR agrees to furnish conceptual product designs, if requested, for the initial product line and all subsequent variations and extensions at no charge to LICENSEE. In addition, if requested, LICENSOR shall assist in the design of packaging, point-of-purchase material, displays and so on at no charge to LICENSEE. However, costs for finished art, photography, typography, mechanical preparation, and so on, will be borne by LICENSEE.

7. QUALITY OF MERCHANDISE. LICENSEE agrees that licensed product(s) will be produced in accordance with the federal, state, and local laws. LICENSEE further agrees to submit a sample of said product, its cartons and packaging material, to LICENSOR for approval (which shall not be reasonably withheld). Any item not specially disapproved within fifteen (15) working days after submission shall be deemed to have been approved. The product(s) may not therefore be materially changed without approval of the LICENSOR.

8. DEFAULT, BANKRUPTCY, VIOLATION, ETC.

A. In the event LICENSEE does not commence to manufacture, distribute, and offer for sale licensed product(s) within _____ months after the execution of this Agreement, LICENSOR, in addition to other penalties that might be available to him or her, shall have the option of cancelling this Agreement. Should this event occur, to be activated by registered letter, LICENSEE agrees not to continue the product(s) development and is obligated to return all prototype samples, drawings, and other materials to LICENSOR.

B. In the event LICENSEE files a petition in bankruptcy, or if LICENSEE becomes insolvent or makes assignment for the benefit of creditors, the license granted hereunder shall terminate automatically without the requirement of a written notice. No further sales of the licensed product(s) may be made by LICENSEE, its receivers, agents, administrators or assigns without the express written approval of the LICENSOR.

C. If LICENSEE shall violate any other obligations under the terms of this Agreement, and upon receiving written notice of such violation by LICENSOR, LICENSEE shall have thirty (30) days to remedy such violation. If this has not been done, LICENSOR shall have the option of cancelling the Agreement upon ten (10) days written notice. If this event occurs, all sales activity must cease and any royalties owning are immediately due.

9. LICENSEE'S RIGHT TO TERMINATE. Notwithstanding anything contained in this agreement, LICENSEE shall have the absolute right to cancel this agreement at any time by notifying LICENSOR of the company's decision to discontinue the sale of the product(s) covered by this Agreement. This cancellation shall be without recourse from the LICENSOR other than for the collection of any royalty payments that may be due him or her.

10. INDEMNIFICATION. LICENSEE agrees to obtain, at its own expense, product liability insurance for at least $2,000,000 combined single unit for LICENSEE and LICENSOR against claims, suits, loss or damage arising out of any alleged defect in the licensed product(s). As proof of such insurance, LICENSEE will submit to LICENSOR a fully paid certificate of insurance, naming LICENSOR as an insured party. This submission is to be made before any licensed product is distributed or sold.

11. NO PARTNERSHIP, ETC. This Agreement shall be binding upon the successors and assigns of the parties hereto. Nothing contained in this Agreement shall be construed to place the parties in the relationship of legal representatives, partners, or joint ventures. Neither LICENSOR or LICENSEE shall have the power to bind or obligate in any manner whatsoever other than as per this Agreement.

12.   GOVERNING LAW. This Agreement shall be construed in accordance with the laws of the state of _____ (your home state). IN WITNESS WHEREOF, THE PARTIES hereto have signed this Agreement as of the day and year written below.

(Signatures and dates here)

This licensing agreement is as brief and plain-speaking as I can make it and still grant you the necessary protections and entitlements, some of which actually derive from omission rather than inclusion. This will become clear shortly. This is a straightforward business agreement designed for you and the licensee, two perfectly intelligent people, to review and negotiate in a friendly, professional manner.

Yes, if the issues are complicated or if there's a great deal of money at stake, you might need an attorney for guidance. However, for routine licensing agreements they're usually not necessary and, frankly, should be avoided if possible. Put opposing attorneys facing each other, and while you and the licensee might have started the meeting as friends, in your eyes he will soon start to look like Adolph Hitler and to him you'll starting to bear a striking resemblance to Osama Bin Laden. Since we want this to be a cordial, ongoing relationship, that's precisely the kind of confrontational atmosphere this agreement is designed to avoid. Let's look at it more closely, section by section.

Rule #7: Avoid putting two lawyers in the same room.

Introduction

The parties to the agreement are identified, as is the product or invention. If there's a patent, the number should be supplied because it is the patent itself that's being licensed. The written description of the product should be accurate enough to identify the product, but not so precise as to eliminate all the derivative products that might spring from the original.

Royalty Payments

The percentage is whatever has been negotiated. Products like giftware and novelties that have small sales but high profit per sale are at a higher level (10 to 15 percent) than appliances or other high volume products where the royalty percentage is much lower (2 to 3 percent). On average, royalties are usually in the 5 percent range. The agreement calls for payments to be made monthly, but the licensee invariably asks for that to be changed to quarterly to eliminate unnecessary bookkeeping.

Also, it's important that the term "net selling price" is understood. Gross sales are what the customer pays to the licensee. However, if the licensee paid the freight or gave the customer some advertising money, it's fair for those costs to be deducted. That's what turns "gross" into "net." However, the licensee cannot deduct things like salespeople's commissions, trade shows, travel, or anything else other than what is specified.

Also, you'll note that this agreement calls for legal fees you incurred to collect due royalties are to be paid by the licensee. If he owes you money and keeps stalling, he's not as liable to yell "So sue me!" when he has to pay the costs. However, note that it works both ways. If he has a legitimate reason for withholding payment and you sue him and lose in court, then you have to pay the legal costs, not him.

Territory

More and more licensing agreements grant worldwide rights because more and more companies are worldwide distributors. What used to be difficult, complicated, and mysterious for manufacturers—selling their products in a foreign country—is now routine. However, if your licensee is not international, or if you have reason not to give him international rights, then Mexico and Canada are considered as part of the local market.

Advance Payment

As with the royalty percentages, the amount of the advance payment is very negotiable. Since there are no rules to follow, you might as well make up your own.

"Max," you ask innocently, "how many of these products do you think you can sell in a year?" Max will offer a number (probably inflated) from which you can do a quick calculation of the amount of royalties that will earn you. "Max, if my figures are correct, that would mean you'll be paying me $50,000 in royalties. Suppose we take just 20 percent of that and make it the advance?" That at least has a sense of reasonable logic to it rather than simply asking for $10,000.

Copyrights, Patents, and Trademark Notices

This is straightforward and will meet with no resistance. If there are trademarks or patents, or patents pending attached to your product, you simply want that information included in the products or packaging so the public can see it. This is for your licensee's protection as well as your own.

Terms and Warrants

Since the products I develop and license are not of a type to warrant a patent, this clause reflects that fact. In other words, once a non-patented product is marketed, it is no longer new and loses its licensing value to anyone else, so the licensee is under no obligation to achieve certain sales or pay certain royalties. I have no power to make him do that because I have no place else to take the product.

However, if your product is patented, then it is the patent itself that's being licensed—and a patent will retain its licensing value if moved from company to company.

Therefore, this agreement can have a time period, after which, if the company has not met certain reasonable, agreed-upon sales goals, you have the right of termination.

Licensing contracts for famous figures like, say, Spiderman, require the licensee's guarantee to pay the licensor a minimum specified royalty every year. They theoretically don't care if the licensee has zero sales; the royalty dollars must be paid in order to keep the agreement and not be sued for payments due.

Also note that this clause says you're to be paid royalties for as long as the company is selling your invention or variations—not 5 years, not 10 years—but forever (or as long as your product remain in the marketplace). Also note that the royalties are to be paid for the original product and all variations and derivatives. Products change over the years to the point where sometimes it's difficult to recognize the original. However, it's still your product, and royalties are still due.

Product Designs

This clause addresses what, if anything you're expected to also do and if you're to be paid for doing it. In my instance, since I'm a designer, it specifies my free contributions and the ones that require payment. It may be that your own idea requires special production techniques, so perhaps you'll need to spend time with the licensee's technical staff or time on the factory floor. Do you do that for free or do you expect to be paid? This is the clause where these matters are addressed.

Quality of the Merchandise

Since your name might be on the product, and certainly your reputation is attached to it, you don't want to see the company selling some junky thing that's ready to fall apart or hurt someone, so you're entitled to sign off on it before it reaches the public. However, this clause says that such approval cannot be unreasonably withheld. You can't halt a product's production because you don't like the shade of purple. However, if you're licensing a fashion product that will have a famous designer's name on it or a series of characters from, say, Disney, then this clause would read differently. These companies have a brand to protect, and so they will have the right to minutely examine everything about the product or garment before allowing it to be released. Since you have no brand to protect, you will probably not have those rights and will need a very good reason to bring production to a halt.

Default, Bankruptcy, Violation, and So Forth

The licensee must have your product on the market within a specified time or else you can cancel the agreement. No contract is open ended; the licensee can't expect you to stand by twiddling your thumbs forever. The company will have agreed to have the product on the market by a certain agreed-upon time, and if the company hasn't done so, you have the right to take your product elsewhere. This happens a lot more frequently than you might think. The company takes your product, pays your advance, and then finds that it can't make it as cheaply as it thought it could, or the market shifted and the product isn't as valuable as originally thought, or competition came out with something better, or the company's sales strategy changed and this product no longer fits in.

All sorts of things can happen between the signing of the contract and the performance date, so you need the right to move on if necessary. Also, if the company finds itself sinking in bankruptcy, there's no reason why you have to go down with the ship. This clause is your lifeboat—it's the kind of escape clause found in any contract.

Indemnification

Picture this scenario. You've invented a terrific new product and licensed it to a Fortune 500 company. Sales are fantastic, and the money is pouring in; the Bentley in your garage is starting to look like a prudent investment. One day, a middle-aged housewife from Bent Elbow, Missouri, claims that the product burst into flames, burned her house down, and inflicted third-degree burns over 40 percent of her body. Oh, yes—and the cat is missing. Three personal injury lawyers are killed in the stampede to her bedside. The surviving lawyer is suing everybody who has ever had anything to do with this vile, evil product, including you.

"But wait!" you say, "Why me? I'm only the humble inventor, I didn't manufacture the product!"

"Tough luck, kiddo," says Snerdley the lawyer. "I'll see you in court. And thanks for the Bentley."

Fortunately this clause requires the company to have at least a $2,000,000 product liability insurance policy with your name on it. Whew! In the litigious world we live in, no company would let a product leave the warehouse without being heavily insured. This policy will surely already be intact, probably for more than the measly $2,000,000, and adding your name to it is a simple administrative matter. But that doesn't mean you can allow it to let it slip by.

No Partnership

Let's suppose you invented a new type of doohickey and licensed it to the Amalgamated Doohickey Company. Things are going fine, and the royalty checks are arriving on time—until one day they suddenly stop. Hey, what happened? What happened is that the FBI discovered that Amalgamated Doohickey is just a front for an international money-laundering scheme, and the guy who signed your licensing agreement, and in fact the entire executive staff, is sitting in jail. This clause confirms that all you know is doohickeys and that your only involvement with these arch criminals has to do with doohickeys and nothing else. This clause is your get-out-of-jail-free card.

Governing Law

Naturally everyone involved in this agreement must add his or her signature and date to confirm agreement with the clauses. However, if the licensee is from another state, it's beneficial to have the agreement say that this contract is in agreement with the laws of your state, not the licensee's. If the case goes to court, having it on your own turf will save you on travel and out-of-state legal expenses, and the hope is that the court might more likely lean on the side of the homeboy than on that of the big shot from another state.

The 10 Nonnegotiable Demands

When union officials meet with management for contract negotiations, the first thing they do is place a list on the table and say with emphasis, "These are our 10 nonnegotiable demands!" then sit back, arms folded, as if to dare anyone to counter them. Management members sit there, struggling to keep smiles from creeping on their faces. They know this is all theater, as does the union team as well. No demands are nonnegotiable in a labor-management meeting; they're simply discussion points.

However, when you meet with a potential licensee to work out the licensing agreement, I believe you *do* have 10 nonnegotiable demands and I do believe they're really nonnegotiable. In fact, these demands are so reasonable that if the licensee doesn't agree to any of them, I think it's time to sit back and reevaluate this potential association. Here they are:

Nonnegotiable Demand #1

The royalty percentage is always based on sales—never profits.

"Hey, we're partners," says the licensee, "whatever profits on this item we make, you get 15 percent." That might sound logical, but don't fall for it. Profits can be creatively interpreted—one way for the tax collector, another for the potential investor, and another for you. Proceed down that road at your peril. Your demand is that royalties are based on sales. Period. Sales are traceable and absolute. Profits are a fairy tale.

Nonnegotiable Demand #2

Sales are sales, period.

There is only one acceptable definition of sales for our purpose: Sales are the monies that a customer gives to your licensee when she purchases your product. Nothing else matters. Some prospective licensees might argue that they should be allowed to deduct things like trade show expenses and salesmen's commissions and catalogs and travel and all sorts of stuff, but you must always say no. That's why they get 95 percent of the proceeds—to have the money to pay for all of those things. All you're getting is a measly 5 percent.

Nonnegotiable Demand #3

Trust, but verify: You must have the right to examine the books.

No licensee would say you can't have access to the sales records; any self-respecting inventor would pack his bags and leave. However, before I amended this agreement, many did balk at the idea that they have to pay my legal fees if I sue them for overdue payments. The fear, I suppose, is that that since they're paying the costs, I might start legal action at the drop of the hat, even though the licensee might have a legitimate reason for withholding fees. That's a reasonable worry, and an attorney gave me the solution. The clause now explains that legal fees are paid by the licensee *only if the suit is successful*. With this addition, the licensee now has no reason to deny agreeing to this clause and you have a right to demand that it stay in.

Nonnegotiable Demand #4

You continue to receive royalties on derivatives of the original product.

Products change over the years, and new products spring from old ones. Today, the board game Monopoly bears scant resemblance to the original, yet royalties are still paid. You have the right to demand that your invention be described in general terms with the specific notation that other products or improvements that spring from it are all part of the family and all generate royalty payments. The only reason a licensee would want the narrowest of descriptions is that he's looking for an escape hatch down the road.

You can't allow that.

Nonnegotiable Demand #5

Royalty payments are forever.

"It's very simple, Ms. Licensee. As long as you're selling my invention and earning profits from it, I expect to be paid my small share. That's the deal. I don't care if it's one year or 20. Payments are based on what you sell, not how long you sell it." Once in a while I run into a potential licensee who wants to limit the time that they have to pay royalties, and in one instance, when I couldn't change his mind, I walked away from the deal. It makes no sense for them to put a time limit on your earning when there's no limit on theirs. I view it as being mean-spirited, and I won't stand for it. I hope you won't either.

Nonnegotiable Demand #6

There is no commitment for legal protection.

This is a tough point, but if you don't listen to me, your restful nights of sleep will be a thing of the past. If the product you've licensed is not patented, you can skip this point—but if it is, listen closely. What you've licensed is your patent, which assumes exclusivity to the licensee. The licensee will logically ask for your commitment to defend the patent and sue copycats or defend the company against some third party who claims patent infringement. Those are reasonable and logical requests, but I'm flat out telling you not to do it. You might not have logic on your side, but fear alone should be enough for you to dig in your heels. I quietly left mention of this out of my agreement altogether and it rarely comes up. But if it does, you need to be prepared.

Voltaire once said that the civil courts twice drove him to bankruptcy—once when he lost the case and the other time when he won it. Patent cases are so expensive, with the outcome never guaranteed, that you can easily spend $250,000 in legal fees in defense of $25,000 in royalties. Since my agreement ducks the issue, there's a good chance it will be overlooked. However, if the licensee brings it up, just tell him that you can't arbitrarily obligate yourself to assume the full burden of legal action if deemed necessary, but if the need arises, the two of you as partners will figure out a way to address it. And then quickly change the subject. Talk about the weather.

Nonnegotiable Demand #7

There must be a nonrefundable advance.

I will never sign a licensing agreement that does not include a nonrefundable advance, and I urge you not to do so either. Sometimes (rarely) you'll encounter a prospective licensee who simply won't pay because, he says, he doesn't believe in advances since it's his money that's being spent to develop and produce the product. If I'm unable to change the individual's mind, then I quit the deal. In some circles, an advance is what's called "earnest money," which is a good description because it indicates the licensee's level of earnestness in going forward. If there's no advance and no penalty for not bringing the product into the marketplace, where's their commitment? If six months into the contract the licensee informs you that the company decided not to go ahead with the product, and if there was no advance, what have you got to show for wasting six months of your time? You should receive an advance large enough to represent a serious commitment, yet not so large as to become a stumbling block. Elsewhere I suggested a formula, but whatever the amount is, don't leave the table without it.

Nonnegotiable Demand #8

There must be a date certain when the product will be on the market.

As you've noticed, my standard contract calls for the product to be ready for shipment no later than six months after the agreement is signed or I have the right to cancel and take the product elsewhere. The advance, of course, is not refunded. This is an arbitrary time period, and I'm willing to be flexible, but there is no contract without this clause. If the product is seasonal—say, a Christmas decoration product—the product has to be available at a certain time that may be longer away than the six-month date. That's fine, but you need a definite date, or the agreement might just languish and you will be powerless to do anything about it.

Nonnegotiable Demand #9

You must be covered by substantial product liability insurance.

I can't imagine any company being in business today without substantial liability insurance, and since adding you by name to its coverage is a minor expense to them, I can't imagine why the company would object. If there is a product liability lawsuit involving your product, lawyers will typically include every name possible to the suit because that improves their chances of collecting awarded damages. Your name as the inventor, even though you had nothing to do with faulty production, will almost assuredly be included. After all, you did sign off on the product, so some responsibility is yours. As unlikely as it may be, if perchance you do find yourself negotiating with a company that doesn't have insurance because it thinks it doesn't need it, my advice is: Don't walk—run to the nearest exit.

Nonnegotiable Demand #10

You must have performance guarantees for patented products.

The type of products I usually create for companies don't require patents, and so this issue is not addressed in my standard agreement. While the savings in not making patent filings are substantial, one of the drawbacks is that I can't demand anything of my licensee, since once my product is on the market, it can't be licensed elsewhere.

I'm stuck with my licensee, for better or for worse—but if your product is patented, that's a different story. The license is specifically for the patent, and since patents keep their value and can be moved from place to place, you have the power to demand in the agreement that if the company isn't performing to minimum agreed-upon levels after a specified time period, you have the right to terminate.

This is a generic agreement that works for me, and I invite you to use it as your own. With a few tweaks it works fine as a template for a software licensing agreement or for licensing an Internet business, as well as for the product invention agreement it was originally created for. You may have special situations requiring special clauses, but regardless of what they might be, you are justified in demanding that each of the aforementioned be included. However, there are other clauses that do require some negotiation, and here's what they are.

The 10 Clauses That Require Negotiation

Negotiable Clause #1

What is the royalty percentage that you'll receive?

This, of course, is the heart of the agreement and has an obviously direct impact on the income you receive from the deal. There are no formulas, but there are some guidelines. Slow-moving, high-profit products pay a larger royalty than fast-moving, low-profit products. Where does your own fit in? Sometimes you might negotiate a lower percentage in the beginning and a larger percentage after certain sales have achieved a certain level, because presumably, the company will have recouped its investment. Sometimes, if competition has forced the company to lower its selling price beyond a certain point, royalty percentages are decreased. This is your job as the licensor: to put your demands on the table. The licensee might disagree and suggest adjustments, but the starting point should come from you. This agreement is your show, not his.

Negotiable Clause #2

What is the extent of the territory being awarded?

The licensee will of course ask for worldwide rights. Why not? However, you might not see evidence that this company is of a size and maturity to be running a worldwide business, and so you might not want to award those rights. You might have your own contacts in Europe, Asia, and Latin America. If you're uncertain, you might give the company world rights but have the non-U.S. market reported separately. If the company doesn't meet certain foreign sales figures, then that market is taken away.

These are all matters that you have to be prepared to address.

Negotiable Clause #3

When are royalty payments to be made?

My agreement calls for monthly payments, and smaller companies usually don't disagree. They pay their salesmen's commissions monthly, so what not pay their royalties in that manner? Larger companies will invariably say that it's too cumbersome to report monthly, and so they'll insist on quarterly payment. I never object, although I do put up a struggle if they want to pay semi-annually.

Negotiable Clause #4

How long must royalties be paid?

If I agree to look for a licensee for an inventor, the deal is that if I'm successful I share in the royalties. Sometimes the inventor will ask how long this split royalty arrangement lasts, and I will reply, "Forever—as long as royalties are being earned."

On occasion you might run into a prospective licensee who will ask the same question, intending for the royalty payments to stop after, say, three or five years. But why should there be a time limit? As long as your invention is creating profits for the licensee, why shouldn't you get your share? Stick to your guns; fair's fair.

Negotiable Clause #5

Is there a minimum performance guarantee? Details?

As explained, if your invented new product does not have a patent, you do not have the leverage to demand that your licensee meet certain goals because there's nowhere else you can take the idea once products are in the marketplace. A company that might have before paid you royalties for it when it was just an idea will now simply knock it off. A patent does give you that leverage, however, and you should exercise it. That you should have this performance clause is nonnegotiable. What is negotiable is the time period and minimum sales requirements that will trigger automatic renewal of the agreement.

Negotiable Clause #6

What additional services are free, and what are to be paid for?

You might possess certain knowledge or skills pertinent to this product that the licensee will want from you. What's free and what's not? In my agreement, I'm willing to provide design sketches for free, but if the licensee wants me to do finished art, then they have to pay for it. You might have similar issues—some services that you'll provide for free and others where you want payment. The licensee might object to the payment part, so some give and take is needed.

Negotiable Clause #7

How big is the nonrefundable advance?

I hope that there should be a nonrefundable advance is a settled issue. The issue that remains is: How large? That answer is: As large as you can get without screwing up the deal. The larger the advance, the larger is the company's commitment to get your product into the marketplace, or the larger the reward to you if they don't. Smaller is never better; larger always is. If you're a genius, then you'll know the precise number to ask for that's just before the licensee says you're crazy and calls for security. If you're not a genius, then proceed with caution. You can usually get a larger advance from a large company than from a small one. The formula I offered earlier is a good starting point; it's reasonable and defensible.

Negotiable Clause #8

What is the certain date for the product to be in the market?

My agreement calls for six months because that's a reasonable time for an average company to bring an average product into the market without putting everyone on overtime. The licensee wants this date to be as far in the future as possible, and you want it to be as soon as possible. What you want is a time frame that puts a sense of urgency in getting the product done and out the door. What you want to avoid is dawdling because the more dawdling there is, the more chance that boredom sets in or the market changes and the product is abandoned.

Negotiable Clause #9

Who pays patent fees to continue work?

If the product being licensed has a provisional patent or no patent at all, and if your licensee would like to have patent protection on it, who pays for the patent work? If the company you're dealing with is a small company, I'm sure they'd say that it's your job to get the patent since you're the inventor. However, you might argue that since the licensee is the principal beneficiary, wouldn't it be fair for the two of you to share the costs? That's not an unreasonable bargaining position. If you're dealing with a large company, they probably have a patent attorney on staff or at least one on retainer, so you can probably get them to pay all the costs. This issue comes up from time to time, so it's best to be prepared to discuss it.

Negotiable Clause #10

Who pays legal fees in the event of a lawsuit, or to initiate one?

This has already been discussed so I won't review it again here. My agreement ducks the issue by not mentioning it (and usually that works), but if the licensee does brings it up, you should be ready to deal with it. Say "no," and obligate yourself to nothing. Stick to your guns, or your worst nightmare might come true. So you know what this clause looks like, here's a sentence that was once inserted into my agreement by a licensee's attorney, which, of course, I promptly removed:

LICENSOR will indemnify and hold harmless from all damages, costs and expenses, including reasonable attorney's fees which may be paid or incurred by the LICENSEE by reason of any claim arising from any breach of LICENSOR'S representation or warranties under this Agreement and LICENSOR, at his own expense, will defend and protect the LICENSEE'S approved use of the product.

There are a few other issues that aren't part of any contract but which might be part of any licensee-licensor relationship, and so they're worth mentioning. There's an old adage in the fashion business that you shouldn't count your profits until you've disposed of your entire inventory. Lots of types of products—fashion products, toys, novelties, gifts, and so on—usually have short, unpredictable life spans. One day the manufacturer is shipping merchandise out the door as fast as he can, and the next day, suddenly, there are no orders at all. When I was a manufacturer, I had items like this, and it's mysterious how that happens—it is as if the whole world becomes bored with the product on the same day. The question for you, the licensor, is: If your licensee has to dispose of many thousands of dollars worth of inventory still in his warehouse by selling it to a closeout guy at sacrifice prices, does he still have to pay you a royalty? Legally the answer is yes. The agreement says you get a percentage of whatever he receives from his customers; it doesn't say if it's from Macy's or Joe the Closeout King.

I take a longer view, however, and I tell my licensee that whatever discount he gave to Joe the Closeout King is the same discount he can take off the royalties. If his closeout discount was 50 percent, then he only has to pay half my regular royalties. I'm in this business for the long haul, and so the relationship is more important to me. If this is going to be a one-shot deal for you, you might decide differently.

Similarly, you and your licensee have signed the agreement and you've banked the advance and gone on your way. Sometime later, in the course of developing the product, it is discovered that a virtually identical product from someone else already exists, and so your licensee has abandoned the project. Does the company get its "nonrefundable" deposit, or is it buyer beware? You did a best effort search before presenting the idea, and your licensee should have done a due diligence search on his own. Does the company get its money back? Legally, I suppose the answer is "no," since no promises were made, so I suppose what matters is how you view the relationship. In my case when this happened, I gave the advance money back without being asked for it. That just seemed like the right thing to do. However, that doesn't mean there isn't justification for you to act to the contrary. I mention it only because these kinds of situations do come up.

Several years ago I wrote a book called *The Amazing Secrets of Millionaire Inventors,* in which I interviewed a dozen inventors from around the country who earned money from their inventions. What I wanted to know is what they did right and what they did wrong that other inventors can learn from. All of their answers were interesting, and some were surprising. To read more, please follow me to the next chapter.

9

LISTENING TO SUCCESSFUL INVENTORS

The winners in life think constantly in terms of I can, I Will, and I am. Losers, on the other hand, concentrate their waking thoughts on what they should have or would have done, or what they can't do.
—Dennis Waitley

The inventors I interviewed for my book *Amazing Secrets of Millionaire Inventors* are a mixed bag—young and old, male and female—with only a few things in common. The first similarity, of course, is that they all had original ideas; and the second is that they all decided to do something about it. The fact that they all persevered and accomplished something despite setbacks and mistakes is of course to be applauded, but what impresses me the most is that they took their ideas under their arms and went out to meet the world. None of these folks hid behind sending letters or opening a website: They got in their cars or planes or trains and went out to meet whomever they had to. Were they nervous? Probably. But so what? Being nervous at the outset makes victory that much sweeter. As author Katherine Paterson noted, "To fear is one thing. To let fear grab you by the tail and swing you around is another."

I asked them all individually what they'd like to pass on to other inventors. What follows are a few of the more common bits of advice.

MAKE SURE YOU REALLY HAVE SOMETHING TO LICENSE BEFORE YOU TRY TO DO IT

Many of these folks, having had no business experience, were unprepared for what it was that they were expected to bring to the table to convince a company president to take on the legal and financial obligations of a licensing agreement. They thought that just having the idea and maybe a little sketch was enough, but they quickly learned differently.

What these folks are saying, and what this book covers in detail, is that in order for your meeting to have a successful outcome, you have to be able to put something into the manufacturer's hands and be able to say words like, "Look at this fabulous new product

I've invented! Look how easily it works! Look at the great things it does!" Inventors are supposed to invent things and prove that what they've invented does what they promise it will. That's why they're called inventors. That's what separates them from dreamers.

Don't Rush to Patent Every Idea You Think Of

This advice comes from a professional, prolific inventor whom I'm friends with, and who has licensed a dozen or more product ideas. He has a system that works for him, and while I don't think it would work for everyone, it is interesting and worth passing on. Since this fellow comes up with useful ideas all the time, he knows how expensive it would be if he rushed to get them patented. He does get a provisional patent, and he does pay an attorney for an opinion letter stating his belief that the product idea is patentable. The inventor then tells his prospective licensee that if a licensing deal is signed, he'll proceed with a full patent filing. If he can't sell the new product idea, his patent investment was modest—a provisional application that he can do himself and an attorney's opinion letter—and if he does sell it, the licensee's advance will cover the filing cost and still leave him with some cash left over.

Get Real: Your Idea Might Be Okay, but It's Not as Hot as You Think It Is

When inventors send me their ideas, they naturally want to impress me with what a big seller it will be. That's fine; that's what they're supposed to do, but often it's clear that they really do not know what they are talking about. Let's suppose the idea is a toothbrush holder that sterilizes the brush while it's being stored. "There are more than one hundred million households in America," the inventor says. "If we just sell to a third of them, that's about 35 million sales. Figure a cost of $20.00—so we have more than $700,000,000 in sales!" Expecting to sell close to a billion dollars worth of toothbrush holders is so unrealistic that it's hard to know how to bring the person down to earth. "But I'm only saying that we'll sell to a third of all the households," he explains as the voice of reason, suggesting that he really thinks it would be more.

That doesn't mean the idea isn't a sensible one (in real life it already exists), but without a realistic perspective of its worth, the inventor's expectations become a stumbling block in any licensing negotiations; in contrast, a defensible enthusiasm could be a wonderful asset.

Know the Field and Find the Need—And Only Then Should You Think About Inventing Something

Rodney Long, a very successful inventor, once told me that when he left his job, determined to make a career as an inventor, he had years of no income. "The problem," as he explained it, "was that I was inventing stuff all over the place. Nobody knew me, and I didn't know anything about all these different industries. I was inventing blind." Finally, Rodney took stock of himself and what he really knew about, and that's where he planted his flag. Rodney knows more about fishing, particularly freshwater fishing, than anyone you'll probably ever meet. When he stuck with what he knew, the inventions and licensing agreements just started to flow and show no signs of stopping. In fact, Rodney has become so well known in the fishing industry for being the originator of innovative fishing product ideas that companies have started coming to him. Rodney is the perfect example of what I try to preach: that inventing is easy (it really is), but that the key to this business is first uncovering what needs to be invented and then filling the need. Knowing what needs to be invented comes a lot easier to folks who concentrate their talents on industries that they already know about and understand.

Find Someone with Brains and Experience Who You Can Talk To

Woodrow Wilson once said that to do his job as president he needed all the brains he had, plus all he could borrow. Whatever path you're taking—inventing a product, creating a software program, developing a new TV game show—there are others who did it before you, or who are in that business. Find one of these folks and learn what he already knows. I like what Admiral Rickover once advised: You should learn from the mistakes of others because life's too short to make them all yourself.

It has been my experience that folks are usually generous with their time and advice if you ask them nicely. You would, of course, have to pay for professional advice from lawyers and accountants, but if you have one person lead you to another, there's a good chance you'll find someone older and wiser who has already done something similar to what you're setting out to do, and who can lead you on your way. Even Bill Gates still thanks his mentors for the valuable advice they gave him when he was just starting out. You needn't tell anyone what your precise idea is, just the nature of it. You can find organized help and mentorship from your local inventors club, or from SCORE, or ask questions on appropriate chat rooms for advice on specific issues. Those might be good places to start. Probably you already know the famous 50–50 rule: "Any time you have a 50–50 chance of doing something right, there's a 90 percent chance that you'll get it wrong." Find a mentor and you'll beat the odds.

Dawdle and You'll Regret It

The inventors I interviewed had lots of stories to tell and lots of tips to pass on having to do with their own experiences. Only a few are mentioned here. Not everyone had the same suggestions to offer, but one thing they could all agree on was that anyone with a great idea who just sits on it is almost guaranteed to regret it. It doesn't matter what the idea is—a brilliant product invention, a clever TV reality show, an innovative software program, or a website business—whatever it is, someone else, somewhere in the world, has almost assuredly thought of the same thing. Is that person sitting on his idea too? You can hope so—but what if he's not?

CONCLUSION

*Will you succeed? Yes indeed, yes indeed,
ninety-eight and three-quarters percent
guaranteed.*

—Dr. Seuss

It's a tough business to dream up a new product or a new idea, for a TV game show or a new software program and have some company pay you for your creativity, but not as tough as you might think. Just about anyone with a thinking mind gets product ideas that might have a financial worth—bus drivers, teachers, brain surgeons, rocket scientists, store clerks—it's not hard to do, and so you might think the competition is terrible. However, when you eliminate all those who have the idea and do nothing about it, you're eliminating a huge percentage. And when you eliminate all those who have the idea and tiptoe out in the world, hoping someone will notice it, you eliminate another huge percentage. So who's left? Who's left are the few hardy folks, like you, who are taking the steps to properly prepare their idea and get themselves in front of someone who can do something wonderful with it.

There aren't many folks like you who are ready to meet the world, and so I'd say the odds for success are pretty good. There are people who are enjoying substantial incomes from licensing their clever product ideas, TV game show ideas, or software ideas—people no better or smarter than you—so why not you as well? I can think of no reason.

"This is a tough business climate"—that's what they always say—"Foreign competition is fierce, the economy is shaky, unemployment is high." That might spell doom and gloom to many, but it means bright skies for those of us who are seeking to profit from fresh, original product ideas. You with the clever idea under your arm are just who these companies, wringing their hands, are looking for. You're the guy on the white horse.

What struggling manufacturing company wouldn't be interested in a brilliant new product to put them back in the black? What software company, fighting fierce competition, wouldn't like some fresh and original program to help them regain distribution? And with so many TV shows tanking, what network wouldn't be thrilled to have something new and wonderful to bring back lost viewers? If your idea or invention truly is fresh, original, and commercially viable, there are executives in companies all over the place who'd love to pay you for it. All you have to do it is find them, meet them, and show them what you have. I know I'm making it sound easy, but it really is a possible dream for those who go after it.

WHY THERE'S NO BUSINESS LIKE THE LICENSING BUSINESS

1. *There is no competition.* There is always room for a great new idea. No one will turn you away because they already have all the wonderful new products they need, or all the brilliant software programs they need, or all the winning TV shows they need. Nobody ever has all they need of something that will earn them more money.

   There is no competition, in the sense that if they take an idea from Mr. X, they can't also be interested in the product inventions or TV show ideas from Mr. Y or Ms. Z. And it's not about price. Who can put a price on a winning new idea?

   In the Introduction to this book I mentioned that I have no hesitation in telling whatever I know about this business for fear that I'd be creating competition, and I meant it. Competition? What competition? All of us together could never satisfy the insatiable demand for great new product inventions, or brilliant new software programs, or new hit TV shows. It never stops! Our economy is so fast-paced that entire industries can vanish in an instant and two new ones can emerge to take their place. Boom times or bust, it makes no difference—great new moneymaking ideas are always needed, and the door is always open if you have one. Can you think of any other business like this?

2. *Virtually no investment is needed.* That's not precisely true because some investment is required, particularly if you're creating a software program. However, compared to the money needed and the high risk involved in starting a new business, the investment in creating and licensing a new idea is within the easy grasp of most of us, and it's hardly a blip on the Risk-o-Meter. I can think of no other business endeavor like licensing where the earning potential is so high in relation to the modest investment and risk involved.

3. *No experience is required.* More than 60 years ago, Charles Darrow, an unemployed plumber in Allentown, Pennsylvania, invented a game called Monopoly and licensed it to Parker Brothers. His heirs are still collecting royalties.

    In 1976, Xavier Roberts, a 21-year-old art student in Helen, Georgia, became interested in fabric sculpture and started making dolls. He came up with the idea of providing birth certificates for each doll he made, and instead of folks buying them, they "adopted" them. The Cabbage Patch Kids were born and licensed to the Coleco Company, becoming the best-selling dolls in the world. In 1984, Mike Bowling, an automotive assembly line worker in Detroit, came up with the idea for Pound Puppies and licensed them to the Tonka Corporation, which sold more than 60 million of them, and they haven't stopped selling yet. In 1986, Rob Angel, a waiter in Seattle, dreamed up a game called Pictionary and licensed it to a game company, and so far more than 40 million sets have been sold.

    An unemployed plumber, a factory worker, a waiter, and an art student—these folks are not rocket scientists; they're just like the rest of us. They were smart enough to have a great idea and, more important, had the fortitude and determination to turn it into something wonderful.

    How many others are there with ideas just as good, sitting on the sidelines?

    There are endless success stories like this, stories about young people and older people, men and women, well-educated folks and those with hardly any education at all. What they have that makes them special is the grit to go out to meet the world and get themselves in front of the right person at the right company to turn their ideas into reality. I'm living proof that you don't have to be a genius to dream up winning ideas. I have two assets on my side that have enabled me to create and license ideas as my business. First, none of this is personal; it's just business. I don't fall in love with my ideas, I don't invest in them emotionally, and I don't take criticism personally. Some of my ideas are wonderful, and some are stinkers—that's just the way it is. I know how to create ideas and I don't expect to ever run out of them. When an idea turns out to be a loser, I chuck it overboard without a thought and move on. Easy come, easy go. And my second asset is that when I do have an idea that I think will work, I know what to do with it to get it to put the royalty checks in my mailbox every month. And whatever I know, I'm happy for you to know it as well.

Years ago I heard former President Jimmy Carter being interviewed. He said that when he was governor of Georgia he thought he had reached the pinnacle of his career. However, his position allowed him to meet a variety of world leaders, and when he came to realize that they were no smarter than he was, that's when he set his political aims higher. Most of us have the tendency to underestimate our own ability while overestimating the ability of others. However, with so many stories of just regular folks who are able to turn their ideas into profit—and some enjoying riches beyond their wildest expectations—it should convince you (if you need convincing at all) that you've got as good a chance of grabbing the brass ring as anyone. So why not reach for it?

4. *The potential is unlimited.* If you go to work as a salesperson for a company and the sales manager tells you that if you work hard the potential is unlimited, what he means is that if you do a good job you can earn a nice living. In licensing, however, unlimited can mean just that—the moon, the stars, and any of the planets you'd like to have. Merv Griffith dreamed up two simple TV game shows—*Jeopardy* and *Wheel of Fortune*—allowing him to live like a potentate for the rest of his life. Isn't your own game show idea just as good? It would be foolish for me to promise you great wealth, although that doesn't mean it's beyond your grasp.

   But if that's not to be, suppose licensing your idea simply adds a nice little cash bonus in the mail every month; doesn't that make the effort worthwhile?

5. *No interruption in your lifestyle.* One of the principle reasons folks don't go into business for themselves, aside from the money risk, is that they like their life the way it is and don't want to change it. They like having time for friends and family,

time for going to ballgames or picnics, and time for a round of golf, and they like the work they do. Becoming an entrepreneur is so all-consuming that there's little time for anything or anyone else. For lots of folks, that's not a worthwhile tradeoff.

Yes, licensing does require an extra effort, but not so much that it will interrupt your lifestyle, and it doesn't require quitting your job or putting your savings at risk.

And best of all, if you're successful in making the deal, the income is passive. There's nothing more you have to do except cash the checks that appear in your mailbox every month. Where else can that happen?

I don't think I have to preach to you about motivation. If you weren't already motivated you wouldn't have taken the time to read this book. What you've been looking for, I believe, is guidance—a blueprint, a plan of action. How do you go from step one to step two? What path should you take? How should you travel it? What should you do and say to achieve your due rewards when you reach your destination? These are the questions I set out to answer, and I hope the information in this book will set you on your way to turning your dreams into reality. As you'll recall from the song Over the Rainbow, Dorothy sang of a place where "the dreams that you dare to dream really do come true." This is the place, and this is your time.

Free at Last!

APPENDIX

This book is deliberately oversized to allow the included forms to be usable as well as useful. I invite you to use any of my own contracts or agreements as your own; and I hope you'll have reason to do so. I've tried not to clutter this Appendix with unnecessary facts and figures and have included only material that I hope will help you achieve success in whatever type of licensing endeavor you've embarked on.

Although every effort has been made to double-check all phone numbers and addresses, I know it's inevitable that some will become obsolete as time passes. In the publishing world, many months can pass between the time a manuscript is prepared and the printed book appears in stores—and of course more months or years can pass before the book winds up in any one reader's hands. Some of the websites that have been recommended might have vanished, some inventor clubs closed or moved, and some forms may have been replaced by new ones. If any of this becomes the case and causes a measure of inconvenience, I apologize and ask for your understanding.

CONTENTS

*These documents can be downloaded from: www.money4ideas.com/Forms0396_x.htm.

LICENSING AGREEMENT

_____ located at _____
(hereinafter referred to as LICENSOR) has given _____
located at _____ (hereinafter referred
to as LICENSEE)

The exclusive production and marketing rights to his new product concept as herein described and as per drawings and/or prototype samples previously submitted. In exchange, LICENSEE agrees to pay LICENSOR a royalty in the amount and under the terms outlined in this agreement.

PRODUCT DESCRIPTION:

1. ROYALTY PAYMENTS: A _____% (_____ percent) royalty, based on net selling price will be paid by LICENSEE to LICENSOR on all sales of subject product line and variations thereof, by LICENSEE, its subsidiaries, and/or associate companies. The term "net sales" shall mean the prices LICENSEE receives from its customers, less any discounts for volume, promotion, defects, or freight. No deductions shall be made for non-collectible accounts, and no costs incurred in the manufacture, sales, distribution, exploitation, or promotion of the subject products shall be deducted from any royalties due and payable by LICENSEE to LICENSOR.

    Royalty payments are to be made monthly on the month following shipment to LICENSEE's customers, and LICENSOR shall have the right to examine LICENSEE's books and records as they pertain thereto. Further, LICENSEE agrees to reimburse LICENSOR for any legal costs he may incur in collecting overdue or wrongly deducted royalty payments.

2. TERRITORY: LICENSEE shall have the exclusive right to market this product line throughout the United States, its possessions, Canada, and Mexico. LICENSEE may do so with any pricing structure and through any legal methods and channels it desires without prior approval from LICENSOR.

3. ADVANCE PAYMENT: upon execution of this Agreement, LICENSEE will make a non-refundable payment to LICENSOR of $ _____, which shall be construed as an advance against future earned royalties.

4. PATENT, COPYRIGHT AND TRADEMARK NOTICE: LICENSEE agrees that on the product, its packaging, and all

Page 2. Date: _____

Agreement between: _____ (LICENSOR)

_____ (LICENSEE)

collateral material, there will be printed notices of patents applied for or granted and applicable trademark and copyright notices showing the LICENSOR as the owner of said patents, trademarks, and/or copyrights under exclusive license to LICENSEE. If not already done so at the initiation of this Agreement, it shall be the responsibility of LICENSEE to make application for these protections if applicable.

5. TERMS AND WARRANTS: This Agreement shall be considered to be in force for so long as LICENSEE continues to sell the original product line or subsequent extensions and variations thereof. However, it is herein acknowledged that LICENSEE has made no warrants to LICENSOR in regard to minimum sales and/or royalty payment guarantees. Further, LICENSOR agrees that, for the life of this Agreement, he will not create and/or provide directly competitive products to another manufacturer, importer, or distributor without giving the right of first refusal to LICENSEE.

6. PRODUCT DESIGNS: LICENSOR agrees to furnish conceptual product designs, if requested, for the initial product line and subsequent variations and extensions at no charge to LICENSEE. In addition, if requested, he or she will assist in the design of packaging, point-of-purchase material, displays, etc. However, costs for finished art, photography, typography, mechanical preparations, etc. will be borne by LICENSEE.

7. APPROVALS: LICENSEE agrees to furnish samples to LICENSOR, free of charge, for his/her approval as to quality and safety; such approval is not to be unreasonably withheld.

8. DEFAULT, BANKRUPTCY, VIOLATION, ETC. In the event LICENSEE does not commence to manufacture, distribute, and sell the licensed products within _____ months after the execution of this Agreement, LICENSOR, in addition to all other remedies available to him/her, shall have the option of canceling this Agreement by so notifying LICENSEE through Registered Letter. Should this event occur, LICENSEE agrees to immediately cease all developmental work and to return all prototype samples and drawings to LICENSOR.

Page 3. Date: _____
Agreement between:_____ (LICENSOR)
                 _____ (LICENSEE)

In the event LICENSEE files a petition in bankruptcy or if the LICENSEE becomes insolvent or makes an assignment for the benefit of creditors, the license granted hereunder shall terminate automatically.

9. LICENSEE'S RIGHT TO TERMINATE: notwithstanding anything contained herein, LICENSEE shall have the absolute right to cancel this Agreement at any time by so notifying LICENSOR in writing of his decision to discontinue the sale of the products covered by this Agreement. This cancellation shall be without recourse from LICENSOR other than for the receipt of any property owned by LICENSOR and for the collection of any royalty payments that may be due him or her.

10. INDEMNIFICATION BY LICENSEE AND PRODUCT LIABILITY INSURANCE: LICENSEE agrees to indemnify, defend and save harmless LICENSOR for and against all damages, costs, and attorney fees resulting from claims, demands, actions, suits, or prosecutions for personal injury or property damage. LICENSEE agrees to cover LICENSOR and his agent as herein named under its product liability insurance with an insurance company, providing protection for itself, LICENSOR, and his agent against any such claims or suits relating to personal injury, product damage, or materials failure, but in no event in amounts less than two million dollars or the limit of the policy, whichever is greater. And within 30 days before manufacture of the product, LICENSEE will submit to LICENSOR a certificate of insurance naming LICENSOR and his agent as insured parties.

11. CONSTRUCTION: This Agreement shall be constructed in accordance with the laws of the Commonwealth of _____.

12. NO PARTNERSHIP, ETC. This Agreement shall be binding upon the successors and assigns of the parties hereto. Nothing contained in this agreement shall be construed to place the parties in the relationship of legal representatives, partners, or joint ventures. Neither LICENSEE nor LICENSOR shall have the power to bind, obligate, or represent the other in any manner whatsoever, other than as per Agreement.

Page 4. Date: _____

Agreement between: _____ (LICENSOR)

_____ (LICENSEE)

13. AGENCY: All statements and sums of money due and payable to LICENSOR under this Agreement shall be rendered and paid to _____, _____ _____ (AGENT), who is authorized to collect and receive such monies. LICENSOR hereby represents and agrees that the receipt thereof by the AGENT shall be good and valid discharge of LICENSEE's obligations in respect thereof and that said AGENT is hereby empowered to act in LICENSOR's behalf in all matters arising out of this Agreement.

IN WITNESS WHEREOF, the parties hereto have signed this Agreement as of the date and year written above.

_____   _____

Licensor Signature   Licensee Signature

_____   _____

Printed Name   Printed Name

INVENTOR'S CONFIDENTIAL DISCLOSURE AGREEMENT

INFORMATION the parties (the party disclosing the CONFIDENTIAL INFORMATION and the party receiving same are hereinafter called "DISCLOSER" and "RECIPIENT," respectively) agree as follows:

1. To be protected hereunder, CONFIDENTIAL INFORMATION must be disclosed in written or graphic form conspicuously labeled with the name of the DISCLOSER as CONFIDENTIAL INFORMATION, or disclosed aurally and be documented in detail, labeled as above, and submitted by DISCLOSER in written or graphic form to RECIPIENT within twenty (20) business days thereafter.

2. RECIPIENT agrees to receive and hold all such CONFIDENTIAL INFORMATION acquired from DISCLOSER in strict confidence and to disclose same within its own organization only, and only to those of its employees who have agreed in writing (under RECIPIENT's own blanket or specified agreement form) to protect and preserve the confidentiality of such disclosures and who are designated by RECIPIENT to evaluate the CONFIDENTIAL INFORMATION for the aforementioned purposes. Without affecting the generality of the foregoing, RECIPIENT will exercise no less care to safeguard the CONFIDENTIAL INFORMATION acquired from DISCLOSER than RECIPIENT exercises in safeguarding its own confidential or proprietary information.

3. RECIPIENT agrees that it will not disclose or use CONFIDENTIAL INFORMATION acquired from DISCLOSER, in whole or in part, for any purposes other than those expressly permitted herein. Without affecting the generality of the foregoing, RECIPIENT agrees that it will not disclose any such CONFIDENTIAL INFORMATION to any third party, or use same for its own benefit or for the benefit of any third party.

4. The foregoing restrictions on RECIPIENT's disclosure and use of CONFIDENTIAL INFORMATION acquired from DISCLOSER shall not apply to the extent of information (i) known to RECIPIENT prior to receipt from DISCLOSER (ii) of public knowledge without breach of RECIPIENT's obligation hereunder, (iii) rightfully acquired by RECIPIENT from a third party without restriction on disclosure or use, (iv) disclosed

by DISCLOSER to a third party without restriction on disclosure or use, or (v) independently developed by RECIPIENT relies as relieving it of the restrictions hereunder on disclosure or use of such CONFIDENTIAL INFORMATION, and provided further that in the case of any of events (ii), (iii), (iv), and (v), the removal of restrictions shall be effective only from and after the date of occurrence of the applicable event.

5. The furnishing of CONFIDENTIAL INFORMATION hereunder shall not constitute or be construed as a grant of any express or implied license or other right, or a covenant not to sue or forbearance from any other right of action (except as to permitted activities hereunder), by DISCLOSER to RECIPIENT under any of DISCLOSER's patents or other intellectual property rights.

6. This Agreement shall commence as of the day and year first written above and shall continue with respect to any disclosures of CONFIDENTIAL INFORMATION by DISCLOSER to RECIPIENT within twelve (12) months thereafter, at the end of which time the Agreement shall expire, unless terminated earlier by either party at any time on ten (10) days prior written notice to the other party.

Upon expiration or termination of this Agreement, RECIPIENT shall immediately cease any and all disclosures or uses of CONFIDENTIAL INFORMATION acquired from DISCLOSER (except to the extent relieved from restrictions pursuant to paragraph 4 above) and at DISCLOSER's request RECIPIENT shall promptly return all written, graphic, and other tangible forms of the CONFIDENTIAL INFORMATION (including notes or other write-ups thereof made by RECIPIENT in connection with the disclosures by DISCLOSER) and all copies thereof made by RECIPIENT except one copy for record retention only.

7. The obligations of RECIPIENT respecting disclosure and use of CONFIDENTIAL INFORMATION acquired from DISCLOSER shall survive expiration or termination of this Agreement and shall continue for a period of three (3) years thereafter or, with respect to any applicable portion of the CONFIDENTIAL INFORMATION, until the effective date of any of the events recited in paragraph 4, whichever occurs first. After such time RECIPIENT shall be relieved of all such obligations.

8. In the event that the parties enter into a written contract concerning a business relationship of the type contemplated herein, the provisions of such contract concerning confidentiality of information shall supersede and prevail over any conflicting provisions of this Agreement. Each party acknowledges its acceptance of this Agreement by the signature below of its authorized officer on duplicate counterparts of the Agreement, one of which fully executed counterparts is to be retained by each party.

Date: _____ Signature (YOURS)

Date: _____ Signature (THEIRS)

SUPPLIER NONDISCLOSURE AGREEMENT

Date _____

This agreement between _____, hereinafter referred to as INVENTOR, and _____, hereinafter referred to as SUPPLIER is entered into under the following terms and conditions.

INVENTOR invites supplier to provide cost information for the following work: To perform engineering work on product concept as per sketches and specifications to be submitted. To enable SUPPLIER to perform this service, it is necessary for the INVENTOR to provide certain secret or confidential information (herein referred to as "Subject Matter") relating to his invention or product concept concerning a _____.

1. SUPPLIER agrees not to reveal, publish, or communicate the Subject Matter to any other party for any purpose without the written consent of the INVENTOR.

2. SUPPLIER agrees to use this information strictly for the purpose of performing his service to the INVENTOR and agrees to hold it in the strictest confidence at all times.

3. All of the work done by the SUPPLIER in connection with the Subject Matter, whether or not patentable, is and shall remain the sole property of the INVENTOR.

4. Upon completion of the assignment, if awarded, SUPPLIER agrees to return all material and objects that may have been provided by the INVENTOR, plus any copies he might have made.

5. If portions of the Subject Matter are already in the public domain, or if SUPPLIER can document that he has prior knowledge of the material from another source, he is not obligated to hold that specific material in confidence.

6. Except for possible exclusions indicated in Point 5, this Agreement shall be in force for five years, commencing with the above date. After this time, the obligations of confidentiality are cancelled.

    This Agreement shall be construed in accordance with the laws of the State of _____ and contains the entire understanding of the parties hereto. IN WITNESS WHEREOF, the parties have indicated their agreement to all of the above terms by signing and dating where below indicated.

INVENTOR: _____ Date: _____

SUPPLIER: _____ Date: _____

Invention Name: _____ Effective Date: _____

AGENCY AGREEMENT

This Agreement is effective (The "EFFECTIVE DATE") as of the date of the last signature below, and is by and between:

THE PARTIES

("The Inventor")

("HRA")   Name: _____
614 South 8ᵗʰ Street
PMB 305   Address: _____
Philadelphia, PA 19147

_____

BACKGROUND

WHEREAS, THE INVENTOR has made an invention, idea, or design that he or she believes has commercial potential, but has not yet successfully commercially exploited it on his or her own, and

WHEREAS, HRA also believes that the invention has commercial potential, and has a great deal of knowledge and expertise in the field of marketing new ideas; and

WHEREAS, HRA is interested in working with THE INVENTOR to commercially exploit the invention, but only on terms of appropriate compensation to HRA in the event the invention becomes commercially successful;

NOW, THEREFORE, THE PARTIES for and in consideration of the mutual covenants hereinafter provided and other good and valuable consideration, the receipt of which is hereby acknowledged, AGREE AS FOLLOWS:

I. DEFINITIONS

As used in this Agreement, the following capitalized terms (whether used in the singular, plural or possessive) shall have the following meanings only:

1.1 THE INVENTION means the technical developments and ideas made by THE INVENTOR that are described in the attached Appendix A.

II. OBLIGATIONS OF AND CONSIDERATION GIVEN BY THE PARTIES

2.1 Agent's Duties

HRA shall:

(a) use its best reasonable efforts to promote and extend commercialization of THE INVENTION throughout the United States of America, and, if opportunities shall arise, in other countries throughout the world;

(b) study and keep under review market conditions to ascertain the most likely commercial partners that might have interest in using THE INVENTION or producing products in accordance with or including THE INVENTION;

(c) at HRA's own expense, prepare or have prepared on its behalf any prototypes, exhibits, demonstrations, or marketing materials that in the reasonable best judgment of HRA may be useful or necessary to advance commercialization of THE INVENTION;

(d) give proper consideration and weight to the interests of THE INVENTOR in all dealings and abide by any reasonable rules or instructions notified in writing by THE INVENTOR to HRA;

(e) not represent any other person whose interests shall interfere with effective marketing and commercialization of THE INVENTION pursuant to this Agreement;

(f) not act in any manner which will expose THE INVENTOR to any liability nor pledge or purport to pledge THE INVENTOR'S credit; and

(g) defray all expenses incurred by HRA in the performance of its duties under this Agreement.

2.2 Exclusivity

(a) THE INVENTOR agrees not to appoint any other person to act as its agent for any duties that would likely overlap or otherwise interfere with HRA's duties under this Agreement during the term of this Agreement from the EFFECTIVE DATE to the expiration date; and

(b) THE INVENTOR agrees that all inquiries received by THE INVENTOR from or through persons other than HRA shall be referred to or notified to HRA, and HRA shall be entitled to the same share thereon as on contracts obtained by HRA.

2.3 Remuneration

(a) In consideration for its service to THE INVENTOR under the terms of this Agreement, HRA shall be entitled to a share on any royalties that are paid or become due to THE INVENTOR or its assigns on the following scale:

(i) Forty percent (40%) on the first $100,000 of royalties accrued in any calendar year;

(ii) Twenty percent (20%) on the remainder of royalties accrued in calendar year.

(b) THE INVENTOR agrees that all royalty payments shall be made directly to HRA. Upon receiving a royalty payment, HRA shall deduct its share and seasonably forward to THE INVENTOR the remainder of the funds received. HRA will make all records pertaining to receipt of royalties on behalf of THE INVENTOR available to THE INVENTOR for inspection and audit purposes upon reasonable notice.

2.4 Confidentiality

THE INVENTOR acknowledges the likelihood that HRA will have to disclose THE INVENTOR to potential licensees and possibly others in the performance of HRA's duties under this Agreement, and that it is likely that many such parties would refuse to accept such information in confidence. Accordingly, THE INVENTOR hereby agrees to release HRA from any previous obligations to maintain information pertaining to THE INVENTOR in confidence.

Notice: Intellectual Property rights may be forfeited as a result of any non-confidential disclosure of THE INVENTOR. HRA encourages THE INVENTOR to explore the possibility of filing parent application(s), provisional patent application(s), or other appropriate protections for THE INVENTOR prior to any loss of rights. At THE INVENTOR's request HRA will provide THE INVENTOR with the name(s) of one ore more registered patent attorneys, which THE INVENTOR will be free to contact at THE INVENTOR's expense.

2.5 Improvements

THE INVENTOR shall own any improvements that are made by HRA to THE INVENTION during the performance of this Agreement.

2.6 <u>Models and Exhibits</u>

HRA shall own any models and exhibits that may be prepared for or by HRA in the performance of its obligations under this Agreement.

2.7 Terms and Cancellation

Either party may terminate this Agreement without cause upon thirty (30) days written notice, although THE INVENTOR may not so terminate this Agreement within the first six (6) months after the effective date of the Agreement. In the event that either party so terminates this Agreement and later enters into an agreement with a business or individual first contacted by HRA, a share shall be payable to HRA according to the provisions of Section 2.3 (a) and (b) above as if the Agreement is still in force.

2.8 Liability

THE INVENTOR shall hold HRA harmless against any liability that may arise in connection with THE INVENTOR

III. MISCELLANEOUS

3.1 **Severability.** If any provision of this Agreement is or becomes or is deemed invalid, illegal, or unenforceable in any jurisdiction, such provision shall be deemed amended to conform to applicable laws so as to be valid and enforceable, or, if it cannot be so amended without materially altering the intention of the parties, it shall be stricken and the remainder of this Agreement shall remain in full force and effect.

3.2 **Governing Law and Jurisdiction.** This Agreement shall be deemed to have been entered into, and shall be construed and enforced in accordance with the laws of the United States of America and the State of Pennsylvania. Any disputes involving this Agreement that for any reason are not subject to aritration as provided in Section 3.7 herein shall be sited in a state or federal court that is located in Philadelphia County, Pennsylvania.

3.3 **Waiver.** No waiver of any rights under this Agreement shall be effective unless contained in a writing signed by the party charged with such waiver, and no waiver of any right arising from any breach or failure to perform shall be deemed to be a waiver of any future breach or failure or of any other right arising under this Agreement.

3.4 **Headings.** Such headings contained herein are included for convenience only and form no part of this Agreement between the parties.

3.5 Costs. In the event of any controversy, claim, or dispute between the parties herein arising out of or relating to this Agreement or the terms thereof, the prevailing party shall be entitled to recover from the losing party reasonable attorneys fees and reasonable costs.

3.6 Integration Amendment. This Agreement constitutes the entire agreement between the parties hereto with respect to the subject matter hereof, and supersedes and voids any and all prior agreements, understandings, promises, and representations made by either party to the other concerning the subject matter hereof and the terms applicable hereof. This Agreement may not be released, discharged, amended, or modified in any manner except by an instrument in writing signed by duly authorized representatives of both parties hereto.

3.7 Arbitration. Any dispute relating to this Agreement shall be decided by binding arbitration by an arbitrator who is certified by the American Arbitration Association and is acceptable to both parties. The site of any arbitration shall be in Philadelphia County, Pennsylvania.

IN WITNESS HEREOF THE INVENTOR and HRA have caused this Agreement to be duly executed on the date first written above

THE INVENTOR

By: _____

Title: _____

HRA

By: _____

Title: _____

DEPOSITORIES—UNITED STATES PATENT AND TRADEMARK OFFICES

Alabama

- Auburn: Ralph Brown Draughon Library (333) 844-1737
- Birmingham: Birmingham Public Library (205) 226-3620

Alaska

- Fairbanks: Mather Library, Geophysical Institute, University of Alaska (907) 474-2636

Arkansas

- Little Rock: Arkansas State Library (501) 682-2053

California

- Los Angeles: Los Angeles Public Library (213) 228-7220
- Riverside: Orbach Science Library, University of California–Riverside (951) 827-3316
- Sacramento: California State Library (916) 654-0069
- San Diego: San Diego Public Library (619) 236-5813
- San Francisco: San Francisco Public Library (415) 557-4500
- Sunnyvale: Sunnyvale Public Library (408) 730-7300

Colorado

- Denver: Denver Public Library (720) 965-1711

Connecticut

- Fairfield: Ryan-Matura Library, Sacred Heart University (203) 371-7726

Delaware

- Newark: University of Delaware Library (302) 831-2965

District of Columbia

- Washington: Founders Library, Howard University (202) 806-7252

Florida

- Fort Lauderdale: Broward County Main Library (954) 357-7444
- Miami: Miami-Dade Public Library (305) 375-2665
- Orlando: University of Central Florida Libraries (407) 823-2562

Georgia

- Atlanta: Library and Information Center, Georgia Institute of Technology (404): 385-7185

Hawaii

- Honolulu: Hawaii State Library (808) 586-3477

Illinois

- Chicago: Chicago Public Library (312) 747-4450

Indiana

- Indianapolis: Indianapolis–Marion County Public Library (317) 275-4100
- West Lafayette: Siegesmund Engineering Library, Purdue (765) 494-2872

Kansas

- Wichita: Ablah Library, Wichita State Library (800) 572-8368

Kentucky

- Louisville: Louisville Free Public Library (502) 574-1611

Louisiana

- Baton Rouge: Troy H. Middleton Library, LSA (225) 578-8875

Maine

- Orono: Raymond H. Fogler Library, University of Maine (207) 581-1678

Maryland

- Baltimore: University of Baltimore Law Library (410) 837-4554
- College Park: Engineering and Physical Sciences Library, University of Maryland (301) 405-9157

Massachusetts

- Amherst: W.E.B. Du Bois Library (413) 545-2765
- Boston: Boston Public Library (617) 536-5400, Ext. 2226

Michigan

- Ann Arbor: Art, Architecture & Engineering Library, University of Michigan (734) 647-5735
- Big Rapids: Ferris Library (FLITE), Ferris State University (231) 591-3602
- Detroit: Detroit Public Library (313) 481-1391

Minnesota

- Minneapolis: Hennepin County Library, Minneapolis Central (952) 847-8000

Mississippi

- Jackson: Mississippi Library Commission (601) 432-4111

Missouri

- Kansas City: Linda Hall Library (816) 363-4600, Ext. 724
- St. Louis: St. Louis Public Library (314) 352-2900

Montana

- Butte: Montana Tech Library of the University of Montana (406) 496-4281

Nebraska

- Lincoln: Engineering Library, University of Nebraska–Lincoln (402) 472-3411

Nevada

- Las Vegas: Clark County Library District (702) 507-3421
- Reno: University Library, University of Nevada–Reno (775) 682-5593

New Jersey

- Newark: Newark Public Library (973) 733-7779
- Piscataway: Library of Science and Medicine, Rutgers University (732) 445-2895

New Mexico

- Albuquerque: Centennial Science and Engineering Library, University of New Mexico (505) 277-4412

New York

- Albany: New York State Library (518) 474-5355

- Buffalo: Buffalo and Erie County Library (716) 858-8900

- New York: Science, Industry, and Business Library, New York Public Library (212) 592-7000

- Rochester: Central Library of Rochester and Monroe County (585) 428-8119

- Stony Brook: Science and Engineering Library, SUNY at Stony Brook (631) 632-7148

North Carolina

- Charlotte: University of North Carolina at Charlotte (704) 687-2241

- Raleigh: D.H. Hill Library, North Carolina State University (919) 515-2935

North Dakota

- Grand Forks: Chester Fritz Library, University of North Dakota (701) 777-4888

Ohio

- Akron: Akron–Summit County Public Library (330) 643-9075

- Cincinnati: Public Library of Cincinnati & Hamilton County (513) 369-6932

- Cleveland: Cleveland Public Library (216) 623-2870

- Dayton: Wright State University (937) 775-3521

- Toledo: Toledo/Lucas County Public Library (419) 259-5209

Oklahoma

- Stillwater: Edmon Low Library, Oklahoma State University (405) 744-7086

Oregon

- Portland: Paul L. Boley Law Library, Lewis & Clark College (503) 768-6786

Pennsylvania

- Philadelphia: The Free Library of Philadelphia (215) 686-5394
- Pittsburgh: The Carnegie Library of Pittsburgh (412) 622-3138
- University Park: PAMS Library, Pennsylvania State University (814) 865-7617

Puerto Rico

- Bayamón: Learning Resource Center, University of Puerto Rico, Bayamón Campus (787) 786-5225
- Mayagüez: General Library, Mayagüez Campus, University of Puerto Rico (787) 832-4040, Ext. 2307

Rhode Island

- Providence: Providence Public Library (401) 455-8027

South Carolina

- Clemson: R.M. Cooper Library, Clemson University (864) 656-3024

South Dakota

- Rapid City: Devereaux Library, South Dakota School of Mines and Technology (605) 394-1275

Tennessee

- Nashville: Stevenson Library, Vanderbilt University (615) 322-2717

Texas

- Austin: McKinney Engineering Library, University of Texas at Austin (512) 495-4511

- College Station: Texas A&M University Libraries (979) 845-2111

- Dallas: Dallas Public Library (214) 670-1468

- Houston: Fondren Library, Rice University (713) 348-5483

- Lubbock: Texas Tech University Library (713) 348-5483

- San Antonio: San Antonio Public Library (806) 742-2282

Utah

- Salt Lake City: Marriott Library, University of Utah (801) 581-8394

Vermont

- Burlington: Bailey/Howe Library, University of Vermont (802) 656-2542

Washington

- Seattle: Engineering Library, University of Washington (206) 543-0740

West Virginia

- Morgantown: Evansdale Library, West Virginia University (304) 293-4695

Wisconsin

- Madison: Kurt F. Wendt Library, University of Wisconsin-Madison (608) 262-6845

- Milwaukee: Milwaukee Public Library (414) 286-3051

Wyoming

- Cheyenne: Wyoming State Library (307) 777-7281

U.S. and Canada
Inventor Clubs

United Inventors Association of the U.S.A.
Rochester, NY
(585) 359-9310
www.uiausa.com

Alabama

Alabama Inventors Clubs
Anderson, AL
(256) 331-5270
e-mail: hubka@nwscc.edu

Invent Alabama
Montevallo, AI
(886) 745-6319
e-mail: Bkoppy@hiwaay.net

Alaska

Alaska Inventors & Entrepreneurs
Anchorage, AK
(907) 563-4337
e-mail: inventor@arctic.net

Inventors Institute of Alaska
Wasilla, AK
(907) 376-5114

Arizona

Inventors Association of Arizona
Tucson, AZ
(520) 722-9545
www.azinventors.org

Arkansas

Inventors Congress Inc.
Dandanell, AR
(501) 229-4515

California

Inventors Forum
Huntington Beach, CA
714-540-2491

Inventors Alliance
Mountain, CA
(650) 964-1576
www.inventorsalliance.org

Inventors Forum of San Diego
San Diego, CA
(858) 451-1028
www.sdinventors.org

Bruce Sawyer Center
Santa Rosa, CA
(707) 524-1773
e-mail: sbdcl@ap.net

American Inventor Network
Sebastopol, CA
(707) 823-3865

Inventors Alliance of Northern California
Redding, CA
(530) 241-5222
www.ideatomarket.org

Colorado

Rocky Mountain Inventors Association
Lakewood, CO
(303) 670-5026
www.RMInventor.org

Connecticut

Christian Inventors Association
Shelton, CT
(203) 426-4205
e-mail: pal@ourpal.com

Danbury Innovators Guild
Danbury, CT
(203) 426-4205
e-mail: iambest@juno.com

Inventors Association of Connecticut
Fairfield, CT
(203) 331-9696
www.inventus.org

Delaware

Early Stage East
Wilmington, DE
(302) 777-2460
e-mail: info@earlystageeast.org

District of Columbia

Inventors Network of the Capital Area
Baltimore, MD
(410) 391-7573
www.dcinventors.org

Florida

Inventors Society of South Florida
Delray Beach, FL
(973) 219-9627
www.InventorsSociety.net

Edison Inventor's Association, Inc.
Ft. Myers, FL
(941) 267-9746
www.edisoninventors.org

Tampa Inventors' Council
Largo, FL
(727) 548-5083

Inventors Council of Central Florida
Orlando, FL
(407) 760-7200
e-mail: erdavidflinchbaugh@bellsouth.net

Space Coast Inventors Guild
Indian Harbour Beach, FL
(321) 773-4031

Tampa Bay Inventors Council
New Port Ritchey, FL
(727) 241-4907
www.tbic.us

Georgia

Inventor Association of Georgia, Inc.
Norcross, GA
(770) 241-4907
e-mail: rreardon@bellsouth.net

Hawaii

Hawaii-International Inventors Association, Inc.
Honolulu, HI
(808) 523-5555
e-mail: sakodaesq@aol.com

Idaho

East Idaho Inventors Forum
Shelly, ID
(208)-346-6763
e-mail: wordinjj@ida.net

Illinois

Inventors' Council
Chicago, IL
e-mail: patent@donmoyer.com

Illinois Innovators & Inventor's Club
Edwardsville, IL
(618) 656-7445
e-mail: Invent@Charter-Il.com

Indiana

Indiana Inventors Association
Marion, IN
(765) 674-2845
e-mail: arhumbert@bpsinet.com

Iowa

Drake University Inventure Program
Des Moines, IA
(515) 271-2655

Kansas

Inventors Association of South Central Kansas
Wichita, KS
(316) 721-186
www.inventkansas.com

Kansas Association of Inventors
Holsington, KS
(316) 653-2165
e-mail: clayton@holsington.com

Mid-America Inventors Association
Kansas City, KS
(913) 371-7011

Kentucky

Central Kentucky Inventors Council, Inc.
Winchester, KY
(859) 842-4110
e-mail: Dlwest3@yahoo.com

Louisiana

International Society of Product Design Engineers/Entrepreneurs
Oberlin, LA
(337) 802-9737

Maine

Portland Inventors Forum
Orono, ME
(207) 581-1488
e-mail: jsward@maine.edu

Maryland

Ray Gilbert
Springfield, VA
(703) 971-7443
www.dcinventors.org

Massachusetts

Cape Cod Investors Association
Wellfleet, MA
(508) 349-1628
e-mail: cdwbauer@msn.com

Inventors Association of New England
Lexington, MA
(781) 274-8500
www.inventne.org

Innovators Resource Network
Shutesbury, MA
(413) 259-2996
www.IRNetwork.org

Worcester Area Inventors
Upton, MA
(508) 529-3552
e-mail: swcel@aol.com

Michigan

Inventors Association of Metropolitan Detroit
St. Clair, MI
e-mail: unc1efj@yahoo.com

Inventors' Council of Mid-Michigan
Clio, MI
(810) 516-8564
http://inventorscouncil.org

Inventors Club of Michigan
E. Lansing, MI
(517) 332-3561

Minnesota

Society of Minnesota Inventors
Coon Rapids, MN
(763) 753-2766
e-mail: PGPENT@yahoo.com

Inventors' Network
St. Paul, MN
(651) 602-3175
www.inventorsnetwork.org

Minnesota Inventors Congress
Redwood Falls, MN
(507) 637-2344
www.invent1.org

Missouri

Mid-America Inventors Association
Kansas, MO
(816) 254-9542

Inventors Association of St. Louis
St. Louis, MO
(314) 432-1291
e-mail: dayjobIASL@Webtv.net

Mississippi

Mississippi SBDC Inventor Assistance
(662) 915-5001
e-mail: blantrip@olemiss.edu

Society of Mississippi Inventors
Brandon, MS
(601) 348-2402
e-mail: gwe2121@bellsouth.net

Montana

Blue Sky Inventors
Billings, MT
(406) 259-9110

Montana Inventors Association
Bozeman, MT
(406) 586-1541

Nebraska

Roger Reyda
Brainerd, NE
(402) 545-2179

Nevada

Nevada Inventors Association
Reno, NV
(775) 677-0123
www.nevadainventors.org

Inventors Society of Southern Nevada
Las Vegas, NV
(702) 435-7741
e-mail: InventSSN@aol.com

New Jersey

Jersey Shore Inventors Club
Freehold, NJ
(732) 407- 8885
e-mail: IdeasBiz@aol.com

Kean University SBDC
Union, NJ
(908) 737-5950
e-mail: mkostak@cougar.kean.edu

National Society of Inventors
Livingston, NJ
(973) 994-9282
www.NationalInventors.com

New Jersey Entrepreneurs Forum
Westfield, NJ
www.njef.org

New Mexico

New Mexico Inventors Club
Albuquerque, NM
(505) 266-3541

New York

The Aurora Club
South Wales, NY
(716) 652-4704

Long Island Forum for Technology, Inc.
Bay Shore, NY
(631) 969-3700
e-mail: LCarter@lift.org

NY Society of Professional Inventors
Farmingdale, NY
(516) 798-1490
e-mail: Dan.weissPE@juno.com

Inventors Society of Western New York
Fairport, NY
(585) 223-1225
e-mail: inventnewyork@aol.com

Binghamton Inventors Network
(607) 648-4626
e-mail: mvpierson@ao1.com

North Carolina

Inventors' Network of the Carolinas
Charlotte, NC
(704) 369-7331
www.inotc.org
e-mail: tgetts@ezclaw.com

North Dakota

North Dakota Inventors Congress
Fargo, ND
(701) 281-8822
www.ndinventors.com

Ohio

Inventor's Council of Cincinnati
Medford, OH
(513) 831-0664
e-mail: InventorsCouncil@fuse.net

Inventors Connection Greater Cleveland
Cleveland, OH
(216) 226-9681
e-mail: icg@usa.com

Inventors Network, Inc.
Columbus, OH
(614) 470-0144
e-mail: 13832667@msn.com

Inventors Council of Canton
North Canton, OH
(330) 499-1262
e-mail: FFleischer@neo.rr.com

Inventors Council of Dayton
Wright Brother's Station
Dayton, OH
(937) 256-9698

Youngstown-Warren Inventors Association
Youngstown, OH
(330) 744-4481
e-mail: rjh@mrnm-Iawyers.com

Oklahoma

Oklahoma Inventors Congress
Oklahoma City, OK
(405) 947-6950
www.oklahomainventors.com

Oregon

South Oregon Inventors Council
Medford, OR
(514) 772-3478

South Coast Inventors Group
North Bend, OR
(541) 756-6866
e-mail: loribdc@ucLnet

Pennsylvania

American Society of Inventors
Philadelphia, PA
(215) 546-6601
www.asoi.org

Central Pennsylvania Inventors Association
Camp Hill, PA
(717) 763-5742

Pennsylvania Inventors Association
Erie, PA
(814) 825-5820

Rhode Island

The Center for Design & Business
Providence, RI
(401) 454-6108
e-mail: cfaria@risd.edu

South Carolina

Carolina Inventors Council
Taylors, SC
(864) 268-9892

South Dakota

South Dakota Inventors Congress
Brookings, SD
(605) 688-4184
e-mail: Kent_rufer@sdstate.edu

Tennessee

Tennessee Inventors Association
Knoxville, TN
(865) 981-2927
e-mail: ialexeff@comcast.net

Music City Inventors of Middle Tennessee
Nashville, TN
(615) 681-6462
e-mail: inventorsassociation@hotmail.com
http://musiccityinventors.com

Texas

Amarillo Inventors Association
(806) 352-6085
e-mail: info@amarilloinventors.org

Houston Inventors Association
(713) 686-7676
www.inventors.org

Technology Advocates of San Antonio
Inventors & Entrepreneurs SIG
(210) 525-8510
www.inventsanantonio.com

Texas Inventors Association
Plano, TX
www.asktheinventors.com

Utah

University of Utah
Engineering Experiment Station
Salt Lake City, UT
(801) 581-6348

Vermont

Inventors Network of Vermont
Springfield, VT
(802) 472-8741
e-mail: comtu@turbont.net

Invent Vermont
Woodbury, VT
(802) 472-874
www.inventvermont.com

Virginia (see Maryland also)

Blue Ridge Inventor's Club
Charlottesville, VA
(434) 973-3708
e-mail: mac@luckycat.com

Washington

Inventors Network
Vancouver, WA
(503) 239-8299

Whidbey Island Inventor Network
Langley, WA
(360) 678-0269
e-mail: wffn@whidbey.com

West Virginia

Inventors Network of Wisconsin
Green Bay, WI
(920) 429-0331
e-mail: intorgb@msn.com

Puerto Rico

Puerto Rico Inventors Association
Saint Just, PR
(787) 760-5074
e-mail: acuhost@novacomm-inc.com

CANADA

Inventors Alliance of Canada
Toronto, ON
(416) 410-7792
www.inventorsalliance.com

British Columbia Inventors' Society
Vancouver, BC
(604) 707-0250
www.bcinventor.com

Inter Atlantic Inventors Club
Dartmouth, NS
(902) 435-5218

Inventors Club of Brantford
Brantford, ON
(519) 753-7735
e-mail: grahamschram@hotmail.com

Women's Inventor's Project
Thornhill, ON
www.womenip.com

PTO/SB/16 (12-08)
OMB 0651-0032
U.S. Patent and Trademark Office; U.S. DEPARTMENT OF COMMERCE
Under the Paperwork Reduction Act of 1995, no persons are required to respond to a collection of information unless it displays a valid OMB control number.

PROVISIONAL APPLICATION FOR PATENT COVER SHEET – Page 1 of 2

This is a request for filing a PROVISIONAL APPLICATION FOR PATENT under 37 CFR 1.53(c).

Express Mail Label No. _____

INVENTOR(S)		
Given Name (first and middle [if any])	Family Name or Surname	Residence (City and either State or Foreign Country)

Additional inventors are being named on the _____ separately numbered sheets attached hereto.

TITLE OF THE INVENTION (500 characters max):

Direct all correspondence to: **CORRESPONDENCE ADDRESS**

☐ The address corresponding to Customer Number:

OR

☐ Firm or Individual Name

Address

City	State	Zip
Country	Telephone	Email

ENCLOSED APPLICATION PARTS (*check all that apply*)

☐ Application Data Sheet. See 37 CFR 1.76   ☐ CD(s), Number of CDs _____

☐ Drawing(s) *Number of Sheets* _____   ☐ Other (specify) _____

☐ Specification (e.g. description of the invention) *Number of Pages* _____

Fees Due: Filing Fee of $220 ($110 for small entity). If the specification and drawings exceed 100 sheets of paper, an application size fee is also due, which is $270 ($135 for small entity) for each additional 50 sheets or fraction thereof. See 35 U.S.C. 41(a)(1)(G) and 37 CFR 1.16(s).

METHOD OF PAYMENT OF THE FILING FEE AND APPLICATION SIZE FEE FOR THIS PROVISIONAL APPLICATION FOR PATENT

☐ Applicant claims small entity status. See 37 CFR 1.27.

☐ A check or money order made payable to the *Director of the United States Patent and Trademark Office* is enclosed to cover the filing fee and application size fee (if applicable).

☐ Payment by credit card. Form PTO-2038 is attached.

☐ The Director is hereby authorized to charge the filing fee and application size fee (if applicable) or credit any overpayment to Deposit Account Number: _____ .

TOTAL FEE AMOUNT ($)

USE ONLY FOR FILING A PROVISIONAL APPLICATION FOR PATENT

This collection of information is required by 37 CFR 1.51. The information is required to obtain or retain a benefit by the public which is to file (and by the USPTO to process) an application. Confidentiality is governed by 35 U.S.C. 122 and 37 CFR 1.11 and 1.14. This collection is estimated to take 10 hours to complete, including gathering, preparing, and submitting the completed application form to the USPTO. Time will vary depending upon the individual case. Any comments on the amount of time you require to complete this form and/or suggestions for reducing this burden, should be sent to the Chief Information Officer, U.S. Patent and Trademark Office, U.S. Department of Commerce, P.O. Box 1450, Alexandria, VA 22313-1450. DO NOT SEND FEES OR COMPLETED FORMS TO THIS ADDRESS. **SEND TO: Commissioner for Patents, P.O. Box 1450, Alexandria, VA 22313-1450.**

If you need assistance in completing the form, call 1-800-PTO-9199 and select option 2.

PROVISIONAL APPLICATION COVER SHEET
Page 2 of 2

PTO/SB/16 (12-08)
OMB 0651-0032
U.S. Patent and Trademark Office; U.S. DEPARTMENT OF COMMERCE
Under the Paperwork Reduction Act of 1995, no persons are required to respond to a collection of information unless it displays a valid OMB control number.

The invention was made by an agency of the United States Government or under a contract with an agency of the United States Government.

☐ No.

☐ Yes, the name of the U.S. Government agency and the Government contract number are: _____

_____

WARNING:

Petitioner/applicant is cautioned to avoid submitting personal information in documents filed in a patent application that may contribute to identity theft. Personal information such as social security numbers, bank account numbers, or credit card numbers (other than a check or credit card authorization form PTO-2038 submitted for payment purposes) is never required by the USPTO to support a petition or an application. If this type of personal information is included in documents submitted to the USPTO, petitioners/applicants should consider redacting such personal information from the documents before submitting them to the USPTO. Petitioner/applicant is advised that the record of a patent application is available to the public after publication of the application (unless a non-publication request in compliance with 37 CFR 1.213(a) is made in the application) or issuance of a patent. Furthermore, the record from an abandoned application may also be available to the public if the application is referenced in a published application or an issued patent (see 37 CFR 1.14). Checks and credit card authorization forms PTO-2038 submitted for payment purposes are not retained in the application file and therefore are not publicly available.

SIGNATURE _____ Date_____

TYPED or PRINTED NAME _____ REGISTRATION NO. _____
(if appropriate)

TELEPHONE _____ Docket Number: _____

Doc Code: Oath
Document Description: Oath or declaration filed

PTO/SB/01 (04-09)
OMB 0651-0032
U.S. Patent and Trademark Office; U.S. DEPARTMENT OF COMMERCE
Under the Paperwork Reduction Act of 1995, no persons are required to respond to a collection of information unless it contains a valid OMB control number.

DECLARATION FOR UTILITY OR DESIGN PATENT APPLICATION (37 CFR 1.63)	Attorney Docket Number	
	First Named Inventor	
	COMPLETE IF KNOWN	
	Application Number	
☐ Declaration Submitted With Initial Filing **OR** ☐ Declaration Submitted After Initial Filing (surcharge (37 CFR 1.16(f)) required)	Filing Date	
	Art Unit	
	Examiner Name	

I hereby declare that: (1) Each inventor's residence, mailing address, and citizenship are as stated below next to their name; and (2) I believe the inventor(s) named below to be the original and first inventor(s) of the subject matter which is claimed and for which a patent is sought on the invention titled:

(Title of the Invention)

the application of which

☐　is attached hereto

OR

☐　was filed on (MM/DD/YYYY) _____ as United States Application Number or PCT International

Application Number _____ and was amended on (MM/DD/YYYY) _____ (if applicable).

I hereby state that I have reviewed and understand the contents of the above identified application, including the claims, as amended by any amendment specifically referred to above.

I acknowledge the duty to disclose information which is material to patentability as defined in 37 CFR 1.56, including for continuation-in-part applications, material information which became available between the filing date of the prior application and the national or PCT international filing date of the continuation-in-part application.

Authorization To Permit Access To Application by Participating Offices

☐　If checked, the undersigned hereby grants the USPTO authority to provide the European Patent Office (EPO), the Japan Patent Office (JPO), the Korean Intellectual Property Office (KIPO), the World Intellectual Property Office (WIPO), and any other intellectual property offices in which a foreign application claiming priority to the above-identified patent application is filed access to the above-identified patent application. See 37 CFR 1.14(c) and (h). This box should not be checked if the applicant does not wish the EPO, JPO, KIPO, WIPO, or other intellectual property office in which a foreign application claiming priority to the above-identified patent application is filed to have access to the above-identified patent application.

In accordance with 37 CFR 1.14(h)(3), access will be provided to a copy of the above-identified patent application with respect to: 1) the above-identified patent application-as-filed; 2) any foreign application to which the above-identified patent application claims priority under 35 U.S.C. 119(a)-(d) if a copy of the foreign application that satisfies the certified copy requirement of 37 CFR 1.55 has been filed in the above-identified patent application; and 3) any U.S. application-as-filed from which benefit is sought in the above-identified patent application.

In accordance with 37 CFR 1.14(c), access may be provided to information concerning the date of filing the Authorization to Permit Access to Application by Participating Offices.

[Page 1 of 3]

PTO/SB/01 (04-09)
OMB 0651-0032
U.S. Patent and Trademark Office; U.S. DEPARTMENT OF COMMERCE
Under the Paperwork Reduction Act of 1995, no persons are required to respond to a collection of information unless it contains a valid OMB control number.

DECLARATION — Utility or Design Patent Application

Claim of Foreign Priority Benefits

I hereby claim foreign priority benefits under 35 U.S.C. 119(a)-(d) or (f), or 365(b) of any foreign application(s) for patent, inventor's or plant breeder's rights certificate(s), or 365(a) of any PCT international application which designated at least one country other than the United States of America, listed below and have also identified below, by checking the box, any foreign application for patent, inventor's or plant breeder's rights certificate(s), or any PCT international application having a filing date before that of the application on which priority is claimed.

Prior Foreign Application Number(s)	Country	Foreign Filing Date (MM/DD/YYYY)	Priority Not Claimed	Certified Copy Attached? YES	NO
			☐	☐	☐
			☐	☐	☐
			☐	☐	☐
			☐	☐	☐

☐   Additional foreign application number(s) are listed on a supplemental priority data sheet PTO/SB/02B attached hereto.

[Page 2 of 3]

PTO/SB/01 (04-09)
OMB 0651-0032
U.S. Patent and Trademark Office; U.S. DEPARTMENT OF COMMERCE
Under the Paperwork Reduction Act of 1995, no persons are required to respond to a collection of information unless it contains a valid OMB control number.

DECLARATION — Utility or Design Patent Application

Direct all correspondence to:	☐	The address associated with Customer Number:		**OR**	☐	Correspondence address below

Name

Address

City	State	Zip

Country	Telephone	Email

WARNING:

Petitioner/applicant is cautioned to avoid submitting personal information in documents filed in a patent application that may contribute to identity theft. Personal information such as social security numbers, bank account numbers, or credit card numbers (other than a check or credit card authorization form PTO-2038 submitted for payment purposes) is never required by the USPTO to support a petition or an application. If this type of personal information is included in documents submitted to the USPTO, petitioners/applicants should consider redacting such personal information from the documents before submitting them to the USPTO. Petitioner/applicant is advised that the record of a patent application is available to the public after publication of the application (unless a non-publication request in compliance with 37 CFR 1.213(a) is made in the application) or issuance of a patent. Furthermore, the record from an abandoned application may also be available to the public if the application is referenced in a published application or an issued patent (see 37 CFR 1.14). Checks and credit card authorization forms PTO-2038 submitted for payment purposes are not retained in the application file and therefore are not publicly available. Petitioner/applicant is advised that documents which form the record of a patent application (such as the PTO/SB/01) are placed into the Privacy Act system of records DEPARTMENT OF COMMERCE, COMMERCE-PAT-7, System name: *Patent Application Files.* Documents not retained in an application file (such as the PTO-2038) are placed into the Privacy Act system of COMMERCE/PAT-TM-10, System name: *Deposit Accounts and Electronic Funds Transfer Profiles.*

I hereby declare that all statements made herein of my own knowledge are true and that all statements made on information and belief are believed to be true; and further that these statements were made with the knowledge that willful false statements and the like so made are punishable by fine or imprisonment, or both, under 18 U.S.C. 1001 and that such willful false statements may jeopardize the validity of the application or any patent issued thereon.

NAME OF SOLE OR FIRST INVENTOR:	☐	A petition has been filed for this unsigned inventor
Given Name (first and middle [if any])	Family Name or Surname	

Inventor's Signature	Date

Residence: City	State	Country	Citizenship

Mailing Address

City	State	Zip	Country

☐ Additional inventors or a legal representative are being named on the _____ supplemental sheet(s) PTO/SB/02A or 02LR attached hereto

[Page 3 of 3]

PTO/SB/18 (08-08)
OMB 0651-0032
U.S. Patent and Trademark Office; U.S. DEPARTMENT OF COMMERCE
Under the Paperwork Reduction Act of 1995, no persons are required to respond to a collection of information unless it displays a valid OMB control number.

DESIGN PATENT APPLICATION TRANSMITTAL

(Only for new nonprovisional applications under 37 CFR 1.53(b))

Attorney Docket No.	
First Named Inventor	
Title	
Express Mail Label No.	

ADDRESS TO:
Commissioner for Patents
P.O. Box 1450
Alexandria, VA 22313-1450

DESIGN V. UTILITY: A "design patent" protects an article's ornamental appearance (e.g., the way an article looks) (35 U.S.C. 171), while a "utility patent" protects the way an article is used and works (35 U.S.C. 101). The ornamental appearance of an article includes its shape/configuration or surface ornamentation upon the article, or both. Both a design and a utility patent may be obtained on an article if invention resides both in its ornamental appearance and its utility. For more information, see MPEP 1502.01.

APPLICATION ELEMENTS
See MPEP 1500 concerning design patent application contents.

1. ☐ Fee Transmittal Form *(e.g., PTO/SB/17)*

2. ☐ Applicant claims small entity status.
See 37 CFR 1.27.

3. ☐ Specification [Total Pages _____]
(preferred arrangement set forth below, MPEP 1503.01)
- Preamble
- Cross References to Related Applications
- Statement Regarding Fed sponsored R & D
- Description of the figure(s) of the drawings
- Feature description
- Claim (only one (1) claim permitted, MPEP 1503.03)

4. ☐ Drawing(s) *(37 CFR 1.152)* [Total Sheets _____]

5. Oath or Declaration [Total Pages _____]

   a. ☐ Newly executed (original or copy)

   b. ☐ A copy from a prior application (37 CFR 1.63(d))
   (for continuation/divisional with Box 16 completed)
   DELETION OF INVENTOR(S)
   i. ☐ Signed statement attached deleting inventor(s) named in the prior application, see 37 CFR 1.63(d)(2) and 1.33(b)

6. ☐ Application Data Sheet. See 37 CFR 1.76

ACCOMPANYING APPLICATION PARTS

7. ☐ Assignment Papers (cover sheet & document(s))

8. ☐ 37 CFR 3.73(b) Statement *(when there is an assignee)*   ☐ Power of Attorney

9. ☐ English Translation Document *(if applicable)*

10. ☐ Information Disclosure Statement (IDS) PTO/SB/08 or PTO-1449
    ☐ Copies of foreign patent documents, publications, & other information

11. ☐ Preliminary Amendment

12. ☐ Return Receipt Postcard (MPEP 503) *(Should be specifically itemized)*

13. ☐ Certified Copy of Priority Document(s) *(if foreign priority is claimed)*

14. ☐ Request for Expedited Examination of a Design Application (37 CFR 1.155) (NOTE: Use "Mail Stop Expedited Design")

15. ☐ Other:

16. If a CONTINUING APPLICATION, *check appropriate box, and supply the requisite information below and in the first sentence of the specification following the title, or in an Application Data Sheet under 37 CFR 1.76:*

☐ Continuation   ☐ Divisional   ☐ Continuation-in-part (CIP) of prior application No.: _____

Prior application information: Examiner _____   Art Unit: _____

17. CORRESPONDENCE ADDRESS

☐ The address associated with Customer Number: _____   **OR**   ☐ Correspondence address below

| Name | |
| Address | |

| City | | State | | Zip Code | |
| Country | | Telephone | | Email | |

| Signature | | Date | |
| Name (Print/Type) | | Registration No. (Attorney/Agent) | |

This collection of information is required by 37 CFR 1.53(b). The information is required to obtain or retain a benefit by the public which is to file (and by the USPTO to process) an application. Confidentiality is governed by 35 U.S.C. 122 and 37 CFR 1.11 and 1.14. This collection is estimated to take 12 minutes to complete, including gathering, preparing, and submitting the completed application form to the USPTO. Time will vary depending upon the individual case. Any comments on the amount of time you require to complete this form and/or suggestions for reducing this burden, should be sent to the Chief Information Officer, U.S. Patent and Trademark Office, U.S. Department of Commerce, P.O. Box 1450, Alexandria, VA 22313-1450. DO NOT SEND FEES OR COMPLETED FORMS TO THIS ADDRESS. **SEND TO: Commissioner for Patents, P.O. Box 1450, Alexandria, VA 22313-1450.**
If you need assistance in completing the form, call 1-800-PTO-9199 and select option 2.

PTO/SB/16 (12-08)
OMB 0651-0032
U.S. Patent and Trademark Office; U.S. DEPARTMENT OF COMMERCE
Under the Paperwork Reduction Act of 1995, no persons are required to respond to a collection of information unless it displays a valid OMB control number.

PROVISIONAL APPLICATION FOR PATENT COVER SHEET – Page 1 of 2
This is a request for filing a PROVISIONAL APPLICATION FOR PATENT under 37 CFR 1.53(c).

Express Mail Label No. _____

INVENTOR(S)		
Given Name (first and middle [if any])	Family Name or Surname	Residence (City and either State or Foreign Country)

Additional inventors are being named on the _____ *separately numbered sheets attached hereto.*

TITLE OF THE INVENTION (500 characters max):

Direct all correspondence to: **CORRESPONDENCE ADDRESS**

☐ The address corresponding to Customer Number:

OR

☐ Firm or
Individual Name

Address

City	State	Zip
Country	Telephone	Email

ENCLOSED APPLICATION PARTS (*check all that apply*)

☐ Application Data Sheet. See 37 CFR 1.76   ☐ CD(s), Number of CDs _____

☐ Drawing(s) *Number of Sheets* _____   ☐ Other (specify) _____

☐ Specification (e.g. description of the invention) *Number of Pages* _____

Fees Due: Filing Fee of $220 ($110 for small entity). If the specification and drawings exceed 100 sheets of paper, an application size fee is also due, which is $270 ($135 for small entity) for each additional 50 sheets or fraction thereof. See 35 U.S.C. 41(a)(1)(G) and 37 CFR 1.16(s).

METHOD OF PAYMENT OF THE FILING FEE AND APPLICATION SIZE FEE FOR THIS PROVISIONAL APPLICATION FOR PATENT

☐ Applicant claims small entity status. See 37 CFR 1.27.

☐ A check or money order made payable to the *Director of the United States Patent and Trademark Office* is enclosed to cover the filing fee and application size fee (if applicable).

☐ Payment by credit card. Form PTO-2038 is attached.

TOTAL FEE AMOUNT ($)

☐ The Director is hereby authorized to charge the filing fee and application size fee (if applicable) or credit any overpayment to Deposit Account Number: _____ .

USE ONLY FOR FILING A PROVISIONAL APPLICATION FOR PATENT
This collection of information is required by 37 CFR 1.51. The information is required to obtain or retain a benefit by the public which is to file (and by the USPTO to process) an application. Confidentiality is governed by 35 U.S.C. 122 and 37 CFR 1.11 and 1.14. This collection is estimated to take 10 hours to complete, including gathering, preparing, and submitting the completed application form to the USPTO. Time will vary depending upon the individual case. Any comments on the amount of time you require to complete this form and/or suggestions for reducing this burden, should be sent to the Chief Information Officer, U.S. Patent and Trademark Office, U.S. Department of Commerce, P.O. Box 1450, Alexandria, VA 22313-1450. DO NOT SEND FEES OR COMPLETED FORMS TO THIS ADDRESS. **SEND TO: Commissioner for Patents, P.O. Box 1450, Alexandria, VA 22313-1450.**
If you need assistance in completing the form, call 1-800-PTO-9199 and select option 2.

PROVISIONAL APPLICATION COVER SHEET
Page 2 of 2

PTO/SB/16 (12-08)
OMB 0651-0032
U.S. Patent and Trademark Office; U.S. DEPARTMENT OF COMMERCE
Under the Paperwork Reduction Act of 1995, no persons are required to respond to a collection of information unless it displays a valid OMB control number.

The invention was made by an agency of the United States Government or under a contract with an agency of the United States Government.

☐ No.

☐ Yes, the name of the U.S. Government agency and the Government contract number are: _____

_____

WARNING:

Petitioner/applicant is cautioned to avoid submitting personal information in documents filed in a patent application that may contribute to identity theft. Personal information such as social security numbers, bank account numbers, or credit card numbers (other than a check or credit card authorization form PTO-2038 submitted for payment purposes) is never required by the USPTO to support a petition or an application. If this type of personal information is included in documents submitted to the USPTO, petitioners/applicants should consider redacting such personal information from the documents before submitting them to the USPTO. Petitioner/applicant is advised that the record of a patent application is available to the public after publication of the application (unless a non-publication request in compliance with 37 CFR 1.213(a) is made in the application) or issuance of a patent. Furthermore, the record from an abandoned application may also be available to the public if the application is referenced in a published application or an issued patent (see 37 CFR 1.14). Checks and credit card authorization forms PTO-2038 submitted for payment purposes are not retained in the application file and therefore are not publicly available.

SIGNATURE _____ Date _____

TYPED or PRINTED NAME _____ REGISTRATION NO. _____
(if appropriate)

TELEPHONE _____ Docket Number: _____

PTO/SB/05 (08-08)
OMB 0651-0032
U.S. Patent and Trademark Office. U.S. DEPARTMENT OF COMMERCE
Under the Paperwork Reduction Act of 1995, no persons are required to respond to a collection of information unless it displays a valid OMB control number.

UTILITY PATENT APPLICATION TRANSMITTAL

(Only for new nonprovisional applications under 37 CFR 1.53(b))

Attorney Docket No.	
First Inventor	
Title	
Express Mail Label No.	

APPLICATION ELEMENTS
See MPEP chapter 600 concerning utility patent application contents.

ADDRESS TO: **Commissioner for Patents**
P.O. Box 1450
Alexandria VA 22313-1450

1. ☐ **Fee Transmittal Form** (e.g., PTO/SB/17)

2. ☐ **Applicant claims small entity status.**
See 37 CFR 1.27.

3. ☐ **Specification** [*Total Pages_____*]
Both the claims and abstract must start on a new page
(For information on the preferred arrangement, see MPEP 608.01(a))

4. ☐ **Drawing(s)** (35 U.S.C. 113) [*Total Sheets_____*]

5. **Oath or Declaration** [*Total Sheets_____*]
   a. ☐ Newly executed (original or copy)
   b. ☐ A copy from a prior application (37 CFR 1.63(d))
      (for continuation/divisional with Box 18 completed)
      i. ☐ **DELETION OF INVENTOR(S)**
         Signed statement attached deleting inventor(s)
         name in the prior application, see 37 CFR
         1.63(d)(2) and 1.33(b).

6. ☐ **Application Data Sheet.** See 37 CFR 1.76

7. ☐ **CD-ROM or CD-R** in duplicate, large table or
   Computer Program (Appendix)
   ☐ Landscape Table on CD

8. **Nucleotide and/or Amino Acid Sequence Submission**
   (if applicable, items a. – c. are required)
   a. ☐ Computer Readable Form (CRF)
   b. Specification Sequence Listing on:

      i. ☐ CD-ROM or CD-R (2 copies); or
      ii. ☐ Paper

   c. ☐ Statements verifying identity of above copies

ACCOMPANYING APPLICATION PARTS

9. ☐ **Assignment Papers** (cover sheet (PTO-1595) & document(s))

   Name of Assignee_____

   _____

10. ☐ **37 CFR 3.73(b) Statement**   ☐ **Power of**
    (when there is an assignee)   **Attorney**

11. ☐ **English Translation Document** *(if applicable)*

12. ☐ **Information Disclosure Statement** (PTO/SB/08 or PTO-1449)
    ☐ Copies of foreign patent documents,
       publications, & other information

13. ☐ **Preliminary Amendment**

14. ☐ **Return Receipt Postcard** (MPEP 503)
    (Should be specifically itemized)

15. ☐ **Certified Copy of Priority Document(s)**
    (if foreign priority is claimed)

16. ☐ **Nonpublication Request** under 35 U.S.C. 122(b)(2)(B)(i).
    Applicant must attach form PTO/SB/35 or equivalent.

17. ☐ **Other:**_____

    _____

18. If a CONTINUING APPLICATION, *check appropriate box, and supply the requisite information below and in the first sentence of the specification following the title, or in an Application Data Sheet under 37 CFR 1.76:*

☐ Continuation   ☐ Divisional   ☐ Continuation-in-part (CIP)   of prior application No.: ....

Prior application information: Examiner _____   Art Unit: _____

19. CORRESPONDENCE ADDRESS

☐ The address associated with Customer Number: [_____]   **OR**   ☐ Correspondence address below

Name	
Address	
City		State		Zip Code	
Country		Telephone		Email	

| Signature | | Date | |
| Name (Print/Type) | | Registration No. (Attorney/Agent) | |

This collection of information is required by 37 CFR 1.53(b). The information is required to obtain or retain a benefit by the public which is to file (and by the USPTO to process) an application. Confidentiality is governed by 35 U.S.C. 122 and 37 CFR 1.11 and 1.14. This collection is estimated to take 12 minutes to complete, including gathering, preparing, and submitting the completed application form to the USPTO. Time will vary depending upon the individual case. Any comments on the amount of time you require to complete this form and/or suggestions for reducing this burden, should be sent to the Chief Information Officer, U.S. Patent and Trademark Office, U.S. Department of Commerce, P.O. Box 1450, Alexandria, VA 22313-1450. DO NOT SEND FEES OR COMPLETED FORMS TO THIS ADDRESS. **SEND TO: Commissioner for Patents, P.O. Box 1450, Alexandria, VA 22313-1450.**
If you need assistance in completing the form, call 1-800-PTO-9199 and select option 2.

Copyright Office fees are subject to change. For current fees, check the Copyright Office website at *www.copyright.gov*, write the Copyright Office, or call (202) 707-3000.

Privacy Act Notice: Sections 408-410 of title 17 of the *United States Code* authorize the Copyright Office to collect the personally identifying information requested on this form in order to process the application for copyright registration. By providing this information you are agreeing to routine uses of the information that include publication to give legal notice of your copyright claim as required by 17 U.S.C. §705. It will appear in the Office's online catalog. If you do not provide the information requested, registration may be refused or delayed, and you may not be entitled to certain relief, remedies, and benefits under the copyright law.

Short Form TX
For a Nondramatic Literary Work
UNITED STATES COPYRIGHT OFFICE

REGISTRATION NUMBER

TX   TXU
Effective Date of Registration

Application Received

Examined By

Deposit Received
One | Two

Correspondence ☐

Fee Received

TYPE OR PRINT IN BLACK INK. DO NOT WRITE ABOVE THIS LINE.

Title of This Work: Alternative title or title of larger work in which this work was published:	**1**	
Name and Address of Author and Owner of the Copyright: Nationality or domicile: Phone, fax, and email:	**2**	Phone ( ) Fax ( ) Email
Year of Creation:	**3**	
If work has been published, Date and Nation of Publication:	**4**	a. Date _____ Month _____ Day _____ Year *(Month, day, and year all required)* b. Nation
Type of Authorship in This Work: Check all that this author created.	**5**	☐ Text (includes fiction, nonfiction, poetry, computer programs, etc.) ☐ Illustrations ☐ Photographs ☐ Compilation of terms or data
Signature: Registration cannot be completed without a signature.	**6**	*I certify that the statements made by me in this application are correct to the best of my knowledge.** Check one: ☐ Author ☐ Authorized agent X _____
Name and Address of Person to Contact for Rights and Permissions: Phone, fax, and email:	**7**	☐ Check here if same as #2 above. Phone ( ) Fax ( ) Email

OPTIONAL

8 Certificate will be mailed in window envelope to this address:

Name ▼

Number/Street/Apt ▼

City/State/Zip ▼

9 Deposit account # _____

Name _____

Complete this space only if you currently hold a Deposit Account in the Copyright Office.

DO NOT WRITE HERE   Page 1 of _____ pages

*17 U.S.C. § 506(e): Any person who knowingly makes a false representation of a material fact in the application for copyright registration provided for by section 409, or in any written statement filed in connection with the application, shall be fined not more than $2,500.

Form TX-Short Rev: 02/2009 Print: 06/2010—50,000 Printed on recycled paper

U.S. Government Printing Office: 2010-357-993/80,084

Copyright Office fees are subject to change. For current fees, check the Copyright Office website at *www.copyright.gov*, write the Copyright Office, or call (202) 707-3000.

Privacy Act Notice: Sections 408-410 of title 17 of the *United States Code* authorize the Copyright Office to collect the personally identifying information requested on this form in order to process the application for copyright registration. By providing this information you are agreeing to routine uses of the information that include publication to give legal notice of your copyright claim as required by 17 U.S.C. §705. It will appear in the Office's online catalog. If you do not provide the information requested, registration may be refused or delayed, and you may not be entitled to certain relief, remedies, and benefits under the copyright law.

Short Form VA
For a Work of the Visual Arts
UNITED STATES COPYRIGHT OFFICE

REGISTRATION NUMBER

VA   VAU

Effective Date of Registration

Application Received

Examined By

Deposit Received

One   Two

Correspondence ☐

Fee Received

TYPE OR PRINT IN BLACK INK. DO NOT WRITE ABOVE THIS LINE.

1 **Title of This Work:**

Alternative title or title of larger work in which this work was published:

2 **Name and Address of Author and Owner of the Copyright:**

Nationality or domicile:
Phone, fax, and email:

Phone (   )   Fax (   )

Email

3 **Year of Creation:**

4 *If work has been published,* **Date and Nation of Publication:**

a. Date _____   *(Month, day, and year all required)*
              Month   Day   Year

b. Nation

5 **Type of Authorship in This Work:**

Check all that this author created.

☐ 3-Dimensional sculpture   ☐ Photograph   ☐ Map
☐ 2-Dimensional artwork   ☐ Jewelry design   ☐ Text
☐ Technical drawing

6 **Signature:**

Registration cannot be completed without a signature.

*I certify that the statements made by me in this application are correct to the best of my knowledge.** Check one:

☐ Author   ☐ Authorized agent

X _____

7 **Name and Address of Person to Contact for Rights and Permissions:**

Phone, fax, and email:

☐ Check here if same as #2 above.

Phone (   )   Fax (   )

Email

OPTIONAL

8 Certificate will be mailed in window envelope to this address:

Name ▼

Number/Street/Apt ▼

City/State/Zip ▼

9 Complete this space only if you currently hold a Deposit Account in the Copyright Office.

Deposit account # _____

Name _____

DO NOT WRITE HERE   Page 1 of _____ pages

*17 U.S.C. §506(e): Any person who knowingly makes a false representation of a material fact in the application for copyright registration provided for by section 409, or in any written statement filed in connection with the application, shall be fined not more than $2,500.

Form VA-Short   Rev: 11/2009   Print: 11/2009—40,000   Printed on recycled paper

INDEX